the spirit YELL*of*OWSTONE

the spirit of YELLOWSTONE

JUDITH L. MEYER
photographs by VANCE HOWARD

ROBERTS
RINEHART

Previous page: Sunset at Great Fountain Geyser

Text copyright © 2003 by Judith L. Meyer
Photos copyright © 2003 by Vance Howard, unless otherwise indicated
Originally published in 1996 by Rowman & Littlefield Publishers, Inc.

Interior design by Piper Furbush

Published by Roberts Rinehart Publishers
An Imprint of the Rowman & Littlefield Publishing Group, Inc.
4501 Forbes Boulevard, Suite 200
Lanham, MD 20706

Distributed by NATIONAL BOOK NETWORK

Library of Congress Cataloging-in-Publication Data

Meyer, Judith L., 1956–
The spirit of Yellowstone / Judith Meyer and Vance Howard.
  p. cm.
    Includes bibliographical references.
    ISBN 1-57098-395-X (pbk. : alk. paper)
    1. Yellowstone National Park—Description and travel. 2. Human beings—Effect of environment on—Yellowstone National Park. I. Howard, Vance. II. Title.
    F722.M49 2003
    978.7'52—dc21   2002156320

The paper used in this publication meets the minimum requirements of American National Standard for Information Sciences—Permanence of Paper for Printed Library Materials, ANSI/NISO Z39.48-1992.

Manufactured in the United States of America.

CONTENTS

Canary Spring, Mammoth Hot Springs

ACKNOWLEDGMENTS

Although she did not serve as one of the "original sources" for *The Spirit of Yellowstone*, my great aunt, Florence Marguerite Meyer, visited Yellowstone National Park as a young woman in 1920. Aunt Florence lived to be 104, and to the end, her eyes lit up and twinkled when she spoke of the park. Her memories transcended space and time, binding her to this park, this place. *The Spirit of Yellowstone* is about creating new memories as much as retelling old ones, and it is about the hope that future generations have the chance to experience and appreciate the place Aunt Florence knew. This book could not have been completed without the help of my family—both immediate and extended. To my parents, Edward and Ilse Meyer: thank you for teaching by example, for your encouragement, inspiration, and assistance. Thank you for traveling with us when we were children and for making sure we stopped and knew a place before moving on. Without you, this project could never have started, progressed, or come to completion. To Aunt Florence and Omi Petersen: thank you for teaching me how important it is to see a place with the heart as well as the eyes. To Carrie, Aaron, and Johanna: thank you for your patience.

Special thanks go to friends and colleagues in Yellowstone who provided help and support during the book's formative years, especially Lee Whittlesey and the staff of the Yellowstone Research Library and Bonnie Sachatello-Sawyer and Joe Sawyer in Bozeman. To Rick Rinehart at Roberts Rinehart Publishers and Erin McKindley at Rowman & Littlefield Publishing Group: many thanks for initiating this edition and all your help and advice in seeing it to fruition.

Further, I wish to thank the National Park Service, the Department of the Interior, and the Northern Pacific–Burlington Northern Railroad for the use of photographs and illustrations in their collections. And, many thanks are due the Wisconsin Cartographic Laboratory in Madison, Wisconsin, for the map of Yellowstone National Park included here.

Finally, I want to thank Bob Pavlowsky for persuading me to finish this project, for sharing my love of Yellowstone and geography, and for our family.

Bull elk at rest

Elk graze near Gardner's Hole

INTRODUCTION

In the spring of 1980, I boarded a Yellowstone Park bus in Gardiner, Montana, and, along with twenty or thirty other new park employees, made the bumpy, gear-grinding journey "up the hill" to Mammoth Hot Springs. Along the way, we exchanged names, points of origin, potential destinations within the park, and glances betraying our excitement and great expectations. Some of us would wait tables or carry bags at Lake Hotel; others would join the "maid brigade" at Canyon Village. I would end up in the Old Faithful area as a tour guide. Like many Yellowstone employees, I came to work in the park for just one season, during summer break from school, to see and do something different, to have an adventure while there were still adventures to be had. I had no idea that, like others before me, I would be drawn back to the park again and again. I had no idea how deeply Yellowstone's spirit would touch my soul.

The Spirit of Yellowstone is about "being taken possession of by the spirit of a place" as a former tourist wrote. It is a study of how the Yellowstone landscape has moved us intellectually, physically, and emotionally. It is also an investigation of those taken possession of: generations of park visitors who, in describing and communicating their experiences to others, created the park as a recognized place.

In welcoming you to the book, I defer to a ranger who wrote about his feelings for the park more than a half-century ago:

> Before leaving Yellowstone I feel that a word is in order regarding what
> I like to term the *spirit* of the place. With all due respect to other

national parks, there is a spirit here that is found nowhere else. It is a spirit born of tradition. Started, perhaps, by the old-time stage drivers that swung their teams over the early roads, or by the guides of forty years ago who originated tall tales of the park phenomena, it is carried on season after season by those who work in Yellowstone during the summer.[1]

Each of the national parks—every place that has meant something to someone—is haunted by its spirit, steeped in tradition, and rich in history, beauty, and wildness. Each one touches us individually and as a nation and therefore deserves our attention, concern, and compassion. For me, however, one park stands out from the rest. In Yellowstone, I have heard the siren's call.

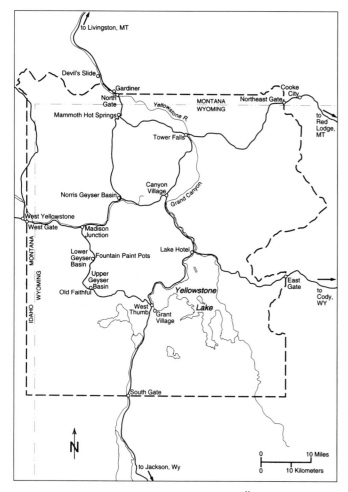

Yellowstone National Park. Courtesy of the University of Wisconsin Cartographic Laboratory

Icicles form around the edges of Tower Falls

Early morning mist rises from the Lamar Valley

REVOLUTIONARY IDEAS
AND EVOLUTIONARY PROCESSES

On 1 March 1872, Yellowstone National Park became the world's first national park. Just a decade earlier, the Homestead Act opened what remained of the public domain to private ownership and settlement. What was it about the Yellowstone region that inspired this novel and revolutionary idea: to remove lands from settlement just when America seemed determined to claim and tame the West? Some suggest it was the park's isolation, distant from population centers and off the beaten trails. Others propose that the strange natural features and the possibility of marketing them prompted their protection. Perhaps the creation of Yellowstone National Park had little to do with geography, politics, or economics at all. Perhaps it was a chance event, the culmination of a history of attempts on the part of the young nation to preserve wild and interesting places.[1]

But there really is something special about Yellowstone, something indescribable—almost eerie—yet very real. It is not only the air, which smells alternately of pine or sulfur depending on where one stands. It is not only the abundance of water—in waterfalls, rivers, lakes, hot springs, and geysers—in an otherwise arid West. Nor is it a particular view, although there are many to choose from: some ugly, some exhilarating, some awe-inspiring. It is the spirit of the place, the whole place, that captivates. To describe Yellowstone by listing its qualities is to do the park an injustice. Yellowstone is more than a recitation of elevations, distances, flora and fauna, geological features, or historical structures. Yellowstone is a "place" with what the Romans called a *genus loci,* or spirit of place: an infectious, irresistible force that stirs something in so many of us.

Almost a century ago, in an attempt to describe the Grand Canyon of the Yellowstone River, a park visitor wrote:

> It is not in singling out each crag and pinnacle, or in separating each bright streak of colour from its neighbor and admiring it alone, that one comes to the fullest appreciation of the grandeur and beauty of the canyon. It is rather in being gradually taken possession of by the spirit of the place, an influence that lasts long after you have ceased to look, a feeling far deeper than the transient delight of gazing on a beautiful picture.[2]

Geographers study this "spirit of the place" by recognizing that some places are more than just locations. They are the focus of people's attention and concern. For some people, the very name of a place can conjure up sights, sounds, smells, even the feel of that place. And just as individual people have personalities—some more endearing, complex, or interesting than others—so individual places can have personalities. "A place is nothing in itself," wrote Wallace Stegner. "It has no meaning, it can hardly be said to exist, except in terms of human perception, use, and response."[3] If this is true, Yellowstone as a "place" is a human artifact. Our shared image of the park is a product of our interacting with, being affected by, and assigning meanings to it.

Over the past century and a half, Yellowstone has changed from a terra incognita, an unknown land, into an international icon of protected and preserved nature. Yellowstone National Park's enabling act was entitled "The National Park," because, like "the" sun or "the" moon, its uniqueness allowed the singular distinction. Today, there are almost 200 units within the U.S. National Park System, and all are Yellowstone's administrative progeny. The park's discovery, exploration, and development have mirrored the growth of the country's appreciation for natural landscapes as well as the birth and maturation of the National Park Service (NPS). National park scholars and enthusiasts commonly refer to this development or maturation as an evolution characterized by America's evolving relationship toward nature more generally. And these three separate areas of concern—Yellowstone, the national park idea, and the National Park Service— are related. As such thinking goes: as attitudes toward nature change, so do—or so should—our attitudes toward the national parks.

This line of thinking has caused the National Park Service to continually adapt its management philosophies and policies to keep pace with the public's ever-changing view of nature. As a result, there has been little consistency over the years in park management. For example, as part of a national "back to nature" movement begun in the 1960s, the NPS changed its century-old, tourism-based management philosophy to one based on restoring and maintaining an "illusion" if not actual state of pristine nature in the parks. As part of this keep-it-natural philosophy, the Service now uses ecosystem management and restoration principles to guide land use decisions. However, national parks are more than representative bits of wild nature. They are deeply humanized landscapes, endowed with meanings beyond those associated solely with their value as ecosystems. And, people's affection for a particular park as "place" may withstand broader societal changes in attitudes toward nature more generally. In other words, people's expectations of a visit to Yellowstone, or Yosemite, or Grand Canyon National Park are not necessarily based only on their attitudes toward nature as a concept. Instead, people's expectations of a particular park experience are tied to that park's image, which has developed in that place over a long period of time. Given the current NPS management philosophy, however, conflicts often arise between what the public has come to expect of a particular park experience and the Service's new and ever-changing ideas about nature and natural systems.

MODELS OF EVOLUTION

Evolution—whether the biological evolution of a species or the cultural evolution of a national park—implies change. But evolution is not uncontrolled, unconditional change. If changes are "evolutionary," they must proceed within the limits of an ancestral form and within certain constraints. Biology's punctuated equilibrium model introduced by Stephen Jay Gould and Niles Eldridge may be useful as a framework for understanding the cultural evolution of national parks. Briefly, "punk eke," as it has come to be known, states that species exist for long periods of time undergoing relatively little change. This is the equilibrium stage, a period of stasis and stability. Eventually, a chance event occurs, the punctuation, which brings about changed environmental conditions favoring the survival of some species over others.[4] With the cautionary note that culture and biology work in very different ways, the punctuated equilibrium model does provide fresh insight to the study of national parks because of the model's emphasis on stasis. Over long periods of time or stasis, national parks develop their unique characters and personalities. Over long periods of time, individual parks become familiar to and beloved by their public.

Generally, stasis is overlooked in favor of the more exciting, controversial, and newsworthy episodes of change. Of main concern in most national park histories are the watershed decisions or dramatic events that altered the course of national park policy. By focusing on change, national park history is typically described as a series of steps or eras, wherein each era is associated with a prevalent societal, political, or scientific trend.[5] Such work is important and necessary to our understanding of the national parks but presents only part of the picture, because it overlooks the importance of what has *not* changed. Despite changes in administrations, governing philosophies, and land and resource management practices since 1872, there is much about Yellowstone that has not changed.

Three other components of the punctuated equilibrium model shine light on our investigation of national park history. First is the importance of initial conditions in influencing subsequent development. Origins are important because they set the stage for all that follows. Second is the idea that evolutionary change occurs as a process of elaboration rather than elimination. Over time, evolution proceeds along lines of both diversity and specialization. As a framework for understanding change in the national

Emerald Spring, Norris Geyser Basin

parks, the punctuated equilibrium model invites us to consider that the meanings we attribute to individual national parks do not necessarily change from one thing to another over time so much as these meanings become richer, more profound, and more specific to each particular park. Third and finally is the misconception of the ideal. Entities—whether an individual, a species, or a particular park—are part of a larger continuum driven not by determinism but by contingency and chance. Each national park is a thing in its own right, a unique place, not a trend progressing intentionally toward some ideal state of national park-ness. Taken together, these four elements of biological evolution theory provide a new perspective on how a spirit of place evolves.

In recent decades, many people have criticized Yellowstone's changeable management policies. Whether the topic is grizzly bears, forest fires, wolf reintroduction, or snowmobiles, Yellowstone's management strategies are often mired in controversy. Currently, Yellowstone is being managed so as to provide an experience of nature rather than of place. And, as public attitudes change, so must Park Service management. Such a guiding philosophy leaves little room for nurturing and maintaining the integrity of the park's spirit of place, something sorely and increasingly lacking not only in Yellowstone but in other grand old parks, the "crown jewels" of the national park system. As Yellowstone's superintendent stated after the 1988 summer of wildfires, the NPS management program is an "uneasy truce between what science tells us is possible and what our value system tells us is appropriate."[6] Adopting a new perspective on the evolution of the national parks—one that releases park management from society's changing ideas toward nature and that acknowledges the importance of people's affection for parks as places—may resolve some of the conflicts and bring about a new appreciation for the national parks and the National Park Service.

YELLOWSTONE'S WRITTEN RECORD

To date, thousands of articles, books, pamphlets, and government reports have been written about the Yellowstone region. The number grows every year as more people visit the park and record their impressions.[7] Similarly, the large number of poems, paintings, sketches, photographs, and even music produced in an effort to describe and honor the park attest to its evocative nature.

The Spirit of Yellowstone is a look at the Yellowstone experience as revealed in written descriptions of the park experience between 1870 and 1991. Since the first generations of tourists provided the germ (or initial conditions) of what became our modern-day image of the park, tourist accounts comprise the largest proportion of sources used here.[8] Included as well are federal government documents such as survey and expedition reports, park superintendents' reports, rangers' field notes, and circulars and notices published by the Department of the Interior and the National Park Service. In the park's first decade, the reports of Ferdinand Hayden figure prominently in molding the public's sense of place, since his expeditions to the park in 1871, 1872, and 1878 led to the publication of a wide variety of materials. State government publications promoting tourism and settlement in the surrounding states of Montana, Wyoming, and Idaho are included as are pamphlets and books published by park concessioners, railroad promoters, and travel agencies. In addition, special attention is paid to the content and format of guidebooks, since such publications enjoyed both high and continuous popularity among park-goers throughout the park's history.

In analyzing these accounts, experiences described by employees were compared with those of visitors, locals with those who traveled great distances, and the wealthy with the less well-to-do. Surprisingly, little variation was found in the various descriptions of the park experience. Overwhelmingly, authors of the earliest accounts were male, a reflection of the times rather than literary biases. Most of Yellowstone's early tourists, reporters, and surveyors were indeed men. Every attempt was made to include women's accounts, but the fact remains that fewer women than men visited the park in its early years, and fewer women than men left written records of their visits during this time. Interestingly, although both men and women apparently took part in typical tourist activities and registered similar reactions, there were differences in how each group behaved while in the park. The diaries and notations of camp life as well as some of the earliest photographs of Yellowstone's tourists indicate that women continued to perform household chores and care for children while en route, whereas men spent more time engaged in hunting and fishing. Hence, although men and women saw the same sights and responded in similar ways to the Yellowstone landscape, their daily routines did differ. An analysis of the literature reveals that along with repeated descriptions of particular locations within the park, six themes appear consistently and prominently: (1) the beauty of the landscape; (2) the uniqueness of the place; (3) tourism and recreation; (4) wilderness; (5) the democratic nature of the park experience; and (6) the park as a place for education.

Beauty: "No greater work of art"

Almost all Yellowstone accounts make mention in some way of the beauty of the park landscape, whether it is a particular scene, a sweeping panoramic view, or the park as a whole. And this aesthetic, visual component appears more often than references to any other aspect of a Yellowstone experience. Visitors seem to have a well-trained sense of what is pleasing to the eye, and comments such as the following are common: "The view from this point was one of the fairest that I have ever gazed upon. It seemed to unite all the elements of beauty—hill, grassy plains, and winding streams."[9]

Much of the language used in the late 1800s to describe the park as beautiful can also be found in writings describing other national parks or nature resorts during that same period and is common to the description of nature as sublime. The idea of nature as sublime describes a human response that combines an appreciation for aesthetic beauty with physical danger or fear. However, although the idea of nature as sublime was a popular literary device of the eighteenth and nineteenth centuries, it lingers on in Yellowstone accounts well into the twentieth century. On one hand, this may simply reflect a familiar way of writing. On the other hand, it may also suggest that references to the sublime were

Bison emerge through the mist in Hayden Valley

for many people for a long time the best means of describing what they really felt: an insignificance or reverence in the presence of Nature or God, an inability to describe accurately the beauty of the scene, or a sense of being moved—often to the point of being physically overwhelmed—by the visual scene.

According to Yellowstone accounts, the park's aesthetic qualities lie not only in majestic, sublime, and dramatic landscapes but also in the more commonplace: "Not only are there scores of grand mountains lifting their craggy sides and rugged summits (few of which have ever felt the tread of civilized man) far up among the clouds, but innumerable sunny glades and shady dells, charming bits of quiet, picturesque scenery, where one will see nothing of the striking, but only the gently beautiful."[10] The park's spectacular scenery moves and inspires its viewers, but the simple and lovely charm of the place touches them as well. Particular mention is made of the classic beauty of Yellowstone Lake with its broad views of distant mountains, watery expanse, and endless shoreline. This soothing scene is then juxtaposed with the almost overpowering beauty of the Grand Canyon and the exhilarating beauty of the geyser basins.

Whether in its grand displays or more mundane views, the beauty of the Yellowstone landscape fosters pensive and reflective moments. Tourists write that they "would go forth to spend another day in contemplation of the wondrous works of the Great Creator."[11] Comments describing religious contemplation or inspiration commonly appear alongside attempts to describe the park's beauty as in a diary entry that reads, "I thank God for creating such scenery and again for permitting my eyes to behold it."[12] Such comments should be expected, since the language of the sublime has strong religious ties. However, the park's scenery elicits religious comments that are not necessarily associated with the sublime. There are many instances of quoting from Scripture, singing hymns, or referring explicitly or implicitly to a Supreme Being, as in this description of the Mammoth Hot Springs: "Just below the large spring . . . is a grove of good-sized pines nearly buried in the sediment, while back of this, up the mountainside where abound the caves and fissures . . . not a half-mile away, are trees a hundred years old, growing on the same formation. Known unto the Great Architect, and to him only, are all his works. His ways are past finding out."[13]

Further, not all contemplative activity is religious. For the Earl of Dunraven, author of *The Great Divide*, a book that familiarized much of England with Yellowstone and the American West, the view from atop Mount Washburn was inspiring in an educational sense:

> It is pleasant thus to gaze out upon the world from some lofty standpoint. . . . It seems to expand the mind; it conducts one by easy pathways down long lands of thought penetrating far into the future of nations, and opens out broad vistas of contemplation through which glimpses of what may be can dimly be discerned. The outlook from such a commanding point elevates the mind, and the soul is elated by the immensity of Nature.[14]

Hence, the theme of contemplation appears in many forms: intellectual, moral, person-al, and religious: "Looking 'through Nature up to Nature's God' can be done easily in this 'Wonderland,' and the overwhelming influence may help one to live better all his life. . . . All of its impressions are grand and enobling in the highest degree,—just the inspiring elements which lift the soul into honor, and beget lofty aims."[15]

For some, the park's beauty provides a setting for quiet, soul-searching contemplation, while in others it instigates a desire for scientific investigation or youthful curiosity. As one tourist wrote of the geyser eruptions, "It was all most wonderful and intensely interesting, giving rise to theories, conjectures, and strange thoughts."[16] Another enjoys just being on vacation and seeing new and different sights: "I spent one of the most profitable hours of my life," writes Alma White while visiting Yellowstone's Upper Falls. "Surrounded by nature in all its primitive beauty and grandeur, I forgot my burdens."[17] A religious or spir-itual element is still evident today in Yellowstone accounts and conversations but is tem-pered with the more secular language and attitudes of modern times.

The Unique: "One imagines that he is no longer in the same country."

Second only to an appreciation for the aesthetic beauty of the Yellowstone landscape is a delight in its uniqueness: the novelty and wonder of this particular place. This theme should not be construed as descriptive of a simple fascination for "singularities," which was part of the attraction of the sublime. Instead, uniqueness describes an appre-ciation for something unique to Yellowstone as a place with a spirit all its own: "Those who may hereafter visit this strange land will bear me out in asserting that a peculiar sensation takes possession of the visitor which can not be dispelled."[18]

Descriptions of the park's uniqueness fall into many categories. One is that Yellowstone is unique because it is so strange, so very different from the landscapes with which most people are familiar. Yellowstone's landscape is uncommon, unusual, and contains "objects more stupendous than the imagination had ever pictured."[19] Especially with their first view of the geyser basins, people admit disbelief and astonishment: "Sitting on our horses we gazed and gazed in silent wonderment at the outstretched world below."[20]

Another aspect of Yellowstone's uniqueness is the variety of its wonders: "Thousands have visited it yearly and have been impressed by the wide range of the phenomena found there. This is one of its great peculiarities. It is, so to speak, many sided in its character. . . . Within a space of about 3,344 square miles [Nature] has concentrated such a variety of objects as one would only expect to find scattered throughout the universe."[21] One Yellowstone guidebook points out all the contrasts to be found in just a single thermal area: "An anomalous feature of this wonderful hot spring system is that pools of different colors lie in closest proximity, each spring being independent of the other, having varying levels at the surface, as well as vary-ing temperatures and pulsations."[22] Another author describes the variety and contrasts of the Fountain Paint Pot area:

Its whole surface is pitted with holes, large and small, in which hot water bubbles and growls, grunts and roars, in every tone of the gamut. Some of the pools are black, others white, and others yellow with sulphur. A choice variety of odors is also observable. . . . In this neighborhood hot and cool pools lay side by side, presenting the most astonishing contrast. Why one stream of water should be boiling while another two feet from it is cold, is difficult to explain.[23]

Not just the thermal areas, but the whole park is a study of contrasts. Stark western peaks rise from "such shady places as fringe the old pastures on the New England hills."[24] In the interior of the park, wide and colorful canyons give way downstream to dark and narrow defiles. At the park's higher elevations, alpine meadows are carpeted with wildflowers and large forests with thick stands of fir, spruce, and pine.

Within this variety are the park's strange juxtapositions. Yellowstone is "a place where there is beauty and ugliness everywhere, peace and chaos, the pastoral and the sublime."[25] Earlier tourists, especially, saw the park as a "rare, multifarious collection of curious and countless samples . . . placed side by side . . . the fair and the foul, the simple and grand, the lovely and revolting, the colossal and the fairy form, and the terrifying and the delightful."[26] Whether simply a reference to Yellowstone's Hell's Half Acre (or any other of the park's place-names associated with the Netherworld) or a comment on the ultimate of contrasts, Yellowstone is truly "ein Bild der Wunder und der Schrecken,"[27] an image of wonder and horror, positioned uniquely between Heaven and Hell.

Tourism: "What a playground for a nation!"

From the time of its inception, Yellowstone National Park was to be a place for tourists. In its enabling act, Yellowstone was described as a public park or "pleasuring ground" as well as a nature preserve. As a result, almost every activity undertaken in the park—from reading the newspaper in the Old Faithful Inn to backcountry hiking—is considered by many to be a tourist activity. For the park's first tourists, one of Yellowstone's unique attractions was the supposedly therapeutic hot spring water, and an image of Yellowstone as a health resort was popular for three decades. Tourists were lured to Yellowstone to "take the cure" by drinking and soaking in the springs' hot water and relaxing at the park's various luxury hotels.

The park's first promoters worked hard to popularize Yellowstone as a place to cure various ailments. The hot waters had a reputation for restorative powers: "Around them had already gathered a number of invalids, who were living in tents, and their praises were enthusiastic in favor of the sanitary effects of the springs. Some of them were used for drinking and others for bathing purposes."[28] Yellowstone's hot springs were repeatedly touted as cures for rheumatism and skin diseases, until these claims were scientifically disproved. Then, promoters focused attention on the invigorating and rejuvenating qualities of the park's high elevation and local climate, which "cannot be surpassed in the world for its health-giving powers"[29] and "pure, bracing air, free from fog."[30] Tourists quickly noted

Winter scene at Midway Geyser Basin

the difference between invigoration and shortness of breath, however, and good-naturedly commented accordingly: "The hotel which we had just left is 6,500 feet above sea-level, but we immediately began to climb to a greater altitude, and soon became aware of the fact that we were getting up in the world."[31] Despite the fact that Yellowstone's popularity as a health resort diminished quickly after the turn of the century, many people went— and continue to go—to Yellowstone today hoping to take part in activities that are presumably healthy because they are undertaken in the out-of-doors. Whether the purpose of the trip is a day hike, a picnic with the family, a backcountry expedition, or to photograph wildlife, tourists flock to Yellowstone to be "out patients" in the Great Outdoors.

It is easier to distinguish between tourism and (outdoor) recreation in the literature of Yellowstone's earliest decades than it is today. Over time, these two purposes for visiting the park have become inseparably linked. "Tourism" assumes there is some form of travel involved. One travels from "home," and both en route and at the destination, one engages in activities that are not standard fare back home. These activities may be arranged specifically for tourists but need not be. "Recreation" can be undertaken at home and away and assumes there is some diversion from the norm that allows the mind and/or body to be relaxed or rejuvenated. Tourists often engage in activities that are both forms of tourism and recreation, such as nature hikes. The act of walking may be recreational, but the idea of traveling to a place that has been set up specifically for hiking makes the activity a form of tourism as well.

For many, the act of traveling itself, being "on the road," constitutes tourism regardless of whether there is an actual destination or not. By the 1900s, describing Yellowstone's purpose in terms of providing recreational activities is almost as common as describing it in terms of tourism. Today, people's perception of what constitutes national park recreation can vary from dangerous, life-threatening, or endurance-testing experiences to viewing a park's features from the window of an air-conditioned touring coach. Nevertheless, if any such activities are undertaken in a national park, they are considered tourism.

Other aspects of the tourism-recreation theme emerge from Yellowstone's literature. For some, Yellowstone is a vestige of the American frontier where tourists can relive the Wild West. In the following, a promoter hopes to convince tourists to enter Yellowstone from Cody, Wyoming, by invoking images of Buffalo Bill: "As you pass the memorial statue erected in [Buffalo Bill's] honor you rejoice in the reality that the West to which he belonged— the West of bison, of wild game, of stream and plain and mountain—is not a thing of the past but lives on perpetually amid the magical splendors of Yellowstone Park, preserved unspoiled always, for the benefit and enjoyment of the people."[32] Still today, the popularity of stagecoach and horseback rides and chuckwagon cookouts attests to people's perception of the park as a place to re-create Wild West days.

Wilderness: "The gravel in the crop of civilization that aids digestion of the whole."

For Americans, the idea of wilderness is an emotional and complicated one, and its tie to Yellowstone is no less complex. The idea of Yellowstone as a wilderness is well represented in the literature, and the very size of the park—its 2.2 million–acre vastness—is an integral part of that sense of wildness. Although millions of tourists pass through the park each summer, many describe feelings of solitude or being alone with nature. Hence, the park's wilderness qualities can be appreciated on a variety of levels. In reality, much of the park really is a wilderness. People routinely get lost, are mauled by wild animals, or die of hypothermia. Further, Yellowstone's features, flora, and fauna are recognized internationally as symbols of wilderness and the wilderness movement. Old Faithful Geyser, grizzly bears, native cutthroat trout, wolves, and bison—each signifies a different motivation or topic of concern within the wilderness movement. As a sacred place, Yellowstone's wilderness takes on a religious quality: "Long may the American people have a tract of country that is not cut up by railroads, telegraph and telephone poles, and given over into the hands of railroad kings. . . . Let the American people fear to desecrate this place, or dedicate it to low and avaricious purposes."[33]

Often, Yellowstone's wilderness is described in patriotic terms that credit the federal government for its foresight and perseverance in preserving and protecting the park: "It is the wildness and grandeur of the enclosing mountain scenery . . . that have raised it to sudden fame, and caused it to be set apart by our national government as a grand national play-ground . . . free to all men for all time."[34] The public applauds the government's decision not only to remove the park from private ownership but also to reassert its claim that Yellowstone is a nation's park: "The Government continues to adhere to its original policy of maintaining forever so far as possible the virgin splendor of the people's great playground. In this it must now and always will have the support and approval of enlightened and patriotic people of every nation."[35]

Yet another wilderness subtheme is Yellowstone as a wildlife preserve: "Geysers are startling, weird, spectacular; the colors of the boiling springs are marvelous; the gay yellows and reds of the strange soft-rocked canyon are exciting; but Yellowstone excited us most of all as a lovely bit of mountain wilderness, where elk and moose and beaver; bison and antelope and mountain sheep, seemed to live as they had lived in pre-Columbian days."[36] Concern for the park's wildlife, however, does not appear in historical accounts until after the turn of the twentieth century, probably because wildlife was until then still considered a culinary treat as much as a visual one. Today, viewing wildlife in a natural, unfenced setting is a major reason for visiting the park.

In Yellowstone, the grizzly bear may not be "smarter than the average bear" but certainly is more than merely another form of wildlife. Yellowstone's "griz" are synonymous with wilderness: "One of the most important parts of the grizzly country experience, besides its rareness, is that hackle-raising humility that comes from knowing one is in the presence of a superior predator. Of knowing that one is, for once, a potential prey species. I hope we never reach the point where we are not allowed to have that feeling." The writer adds, however, that "being mauled by a grizzly bear has always struck me as one of those wilderness experiences where the novelty wears off almost right away."[37]

Young black bear in autumn

The grizzlies' presence in Yellowstone nowadays is considered proof of Yellowstone's wildness, and the size of the park's bear population is often used as an indicator of Yellowstone's ecological health. However, threads of ecological thought have always been present in people's perceptions of the park, although not in such numbers as wilderness proponents of today might wish. Ecology appears as an early and sustained theme that suggests that people have long recognized ecological principles and the need to protect entire ecosystems. In the following, the author describes the open valleys between mountains: "They are not only beautiful but useful, and answer a very wise purpose in the economy of Nature, for, acting like huge reservoirs, they collect the thousand rills that steal out from under the everlasting snows, and uniting them in one perennial stream launch it out into the world to bear fertility to the arid plains below."[38]

Sophisticated, scientific knowledge of the interdependence among different species and between organisms and their physical environments was not available a century ago, but people were aware of the "interconnectedness" of the natural world. Early accounts tell of the need to protect both Yellowstone's forests and the forested areas surrounding the park. People understood the park's value as wildlife habitat and as a reservoir: "The whole region is covered with a thick forest growth cutting off the intense rays of the summer sun, and covering the ground with a vegetable mold through which the surface waters filter but slowly. It is a conservative estimate . . . that these forests prolong the melting of the snows from four to six weeks."[39]

The current dilemma of reconciling the ideals of wilderness preservation with the realities of tourism is not a new one. People have long expressed both approval and disappointment in the management of the park's wilderness areas. In general, however, much of Yellowstone's public is satisfied with the park's gentrified wilderness:

> It is hardly safe in these days to define a wilderness, it contains so much that is unexpected. We must refuse to be convinced by the unsatisfied one who finds incongruity in the ugly red hotels, the yellow coaches, the galloping tourists, the kodaks. After all, every age is entitled to its own sort of wilderness, and ours seems to include the tourist and the hotel; the traveler is to-day as much a part of the Rocky Mountains as the elk or the lodge-pole pine. No picture of the modern wilderness would to-day be complete without the sturdy gold-skirted American girl with her Kodak, the white-top wagon, the Eastern youth turned suddenly Western, with oddly worn sombrero and spurs.[40]

Most people believe that nature and people can and should coexist in the park, if only because of its great size. Yellowstone's record suggests that there is room enough for both wilderness purists and those who enjoy a more civilized wilderness experience:

Behind us lay a week of luxurious sight-seeing in Yellowstone Park—the civilized part of it, thick with hotels, camps, and campers, autos and tourists. Before us lay alluring weeks of the open trail in the country to the south, within the Park and out of it—a blessed country of no roads, and few visitors. An undisturbed fairyland of mountains, rivers and forests, all populated with wild life like a vast unfettered zoo.[41]

Democracy: "Maintained by the Nation for the People"

Yellowstone tourists have persistently written about their sense of pride in the American government for its role in establishing the park. These statements may have been part and parcel of the nationalistic fervor of the post–Civil War era. American nature writing of the late nineteenth century as well as promotional material associated with the opening of the American West is full of pro-America slogans and sentiments. By the early 1870s, at the time of Yellowstone's establishment, Americans were still creating a new mythology for themselves and a combination of religion, patriotism, and the idea of nature as sublime permeated popular literature. The American public, it seemed, wanted to believe in the country's divinely ordained success, and Yellowstone's discovery and establishment as a national park went hand in hand with such beliefs. John Stoddard, essayist, world traveler, and prominent lecturer, typifies this period and mind-set in his description of Eagle's Nest Rock near the north entrance of the park:

> On three sides this is guarded by lofty, well-nigh inaccessible mountains, as though the Infinite Himself would not allow mankind to rashly enter its sublime enclosure. In this respect our Government has wisely imitated the Creator. It has proclaimed to all the world the sanctity of this peculiar area. It has received it as a gift from God and, as His trustee, holds it for the welfare of humanity.[42]

A sense of nationalism can be found in the use of Gothic architectural terms when comparing the park's geologic features to European castles and cathedrals:

> Gothic arches, Corinthian capitals and Egyptian basilicas built before human architecture was born . . . Gibraltars and Sebastopols that never can be taken; Alhambras, where kings of strength and queens of beauty reigned long before the first earthly crown was empearled . . . a new and divinely inspired revelation, the Old Testament written on papyrus, the New Testament written on parchment, and now this Last Testament written on the rocks.[43]

Repeatedly, the size, shape, beauty, and antiquity of Yellowstone's natural landscapes are compared to both natural and built features of Europe. One magazine editor even

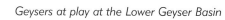

Geysers at play at the Lower Geyser Basin

capitalized on the use of superlatives and patriotic language in Yellowstone descriptions to poke fun at these comparisons:

> Why should we waste ourselves in unpatriotic wonderment over the gorge of the Tamina or the Via Mala, when nature has furnished us with the Grand Cañon of the Yellowstone, in which the famed Swiss ravines would be but as a crevice or a wrinkle? Why run across the sea to stifle and sneeze over the ill odors of Solfaterra, when we can spoil our lungs or our trowsers to better effect, and on an incomparably larger scale, with the gigantic boiling springs and geysers of Montana?[44]

Certainly, the owners of westward-expanding railroads and some politicians had ulterior motives for using nationalistic language in promoting the establishment of national parks. For most park visitors, however, these comparisons to Europe were used because these were familiar terms in common use and presented the best means of communicating the dimensions and impact of the landscape.

As in the wilderness theme, democracy is often used to voice approval and recognition of the federal government's commitment to protect and preserve Yellowstone for all people. After viewing an eruption of Castle Geyser, John Stoddard wrote: "I realized then, as never before the noble action of our Government in giving his incomparable region to the people . . . thanks to the generosity of Congress, the Park itself, and everything that it contains, are absolutely free to all, rich and poor, native and foreigner,—forever consecrated to the education and delight of man."[45]

The idea of democracy finds one of its strongest expressions in comments about the demographic mix of Yellowstone tourists. Park literature is full of comments describing the variety of people who come to the park:

> The jolly tourists who hail from every corner of the globe . . . are all imbued with the happy-go-lucky, get-there-quick American spirit. Among them we find a Chinese doctor, an African missionary, a Spanish opera star, several titled Englishmen, merry school teachers bound for a joyous holiday away from the crowded schoolrooms; lawyers who seek diversion from the humdrums of the courts . . . all making up a happy band of pilgrims, bound for the wonderland of the Yellowstone.[46]

Tourists are characterized not only by their nationality, background, and reason for travel, but by their varied social and economic status as well. In the park, "A man's dress gave no clue to his vocation or social position. The wearer of a dilapidated hat, ancient blouse and trowsers showing signs of frequent acquaintance with the saddle, was a U.S. Engineer officer in

charge of a construction party. His far better clothed companion was one of his teamsters."[47]

Signs of an appreciation for the diversity of tourists are recognized still today as a ranger describes the temporary residents of a Yellowstone campground on a typical summer evening: "Next to the forty-thousand-dollar mobile home laden with dignified retirees is a literal commune of one- or two-person tents, suffused in a light haze of illegal smoke and heavy music. Next to the Mormons, the Episcopalians; the Democrats, the Birchers; the gun nuts, the bleeding hearts. It's not a melting pot, but it's a hell of a mixing bowl."[48] As a uniquely American institution—as a park for the masses—Yellowstone National Park is a recognized success:

> In the flush of the moment, I began to think of this park as the repository of things American. It is a place where we can be free: free from the telephone, free to climb a mountain, free from structure, free to fish, free from urban noise, free to cook on a campfire, free from the clock, free to do nothing . . . I couldn't help think, as I drove home to my cabin, that freedom runs as a thread in this park.[49]

Education: "For the benefit and instruction of the people"

At first glance, education seems less complex a theme than many aforementioned ones. However, people have understood Yellowstone to be a place to learn in a wide variety of ways. An educational trip to Yellowstone can be seen as "the ideal summer school of nature study" as well as a place to learn moral and civic lessons.[50] John Muir, a strong voice early on for the value of an outdoor education, believed the national parks to be "universities without walls." In writing of Yellowstone, Muir encouraged people to "take a look into a few of the tertiary volumes of the grand geological library of the park, and see how God writes history. No technical knowledge is required; only a calm day and a calm mind . . . a wonderful set of volumes lying on their sides,— books a million years old, well bound, miles in size, with full page illustrations."[51]

People continue to view the Yellowstone experience as an educational one. A former interpretive ranger reports, "Many people come to us already fired up about the park, and we get to deal with them when they are most receptive to new ideas, most willing to be taught."[52] However, the park's literary record indicates that today there is less individually motivated learning and more reliance on being taught by others. Many tourists wishing to learn about the park participate in organized activities by joining ranger-led nature walks and talks, watching educational films in the visitor centers, examining museum displays, or taking part in summer field schools.

Education is not mentioned as frequently as other elements of a Yellowstone experience, although its counterpart—the use of the park for science and scientific investigation— figures quite prominently during the park's first few decades.

Already at the time of the park's discovery, its value to science was noted: "I returned to camp in the evening profoundly impressed with the greatness of the phenomena we

Aspen leaves in autumn

Morning mist in Hayden Valley

were witnessing from day to day, and of their probable future importance to science, in unraveling mysteries hitherto unsolvable."[53] The very creation of the park was heralded as "a tribute from our legislators to science, and the gratitude of the nation of men of science in all parts of the world is due them for this munificent donation."[54]

One educational activity that has become an institution is the campfire program. Sitting around a campfire while a ranger interprets the park is a wonderful blend of many of the park's traditions. It combines an element of wilderness recreation with an aura of the Wild West, the camaraderie of democratic tourism, and a chance to learn about the park:

> I feel about campfire programs the same way I feel about rangers. Whatever happens to the parks, whatever political ills befall them, this faltering institution—the old campfire circle—simply must go on. Even when bloated and electronically sterilized, it is one of the unexpected blessings of a visit to Yellowstone, a touch of what's best about sharing the woods. Philosophers emphasize the solitariness of wilderness experience, and I approve; the renewal and stimulation to be had alone with nature is priceless. But national parks are more than wilderness. They are outposts on the edges, from which people can go, or at least peer, in. And the outposts, be they campgrounds, museums, or even hotels, can be enriching . . . And, if the ranger is any good at his work, if the fire crackles and crumbles hospitably as they sit, and if the smoke that stings their eyes that night surprises them a few days later when they next put that coat on, their Yellowstone campfire will never go out.[55]

In the one-and-a-quarter centuries since Yellowstone's establishment, the world, the United States, the National Park Service, and Yellowstone itself have undergone many changes, some more disruptive and unsettling than others. In this atmosphere of change, however, an image of Yellowstone as a unique place has persisted, and this image is one of tradition. All of the themes mentioned above—an appreciation for the park's beauty, its uniqueness, its opportunities for tourism and recreation, its wildness, democratic ownership, and educational qualities—have all persisted over time. Yellowstone's evolution has not been one of haphazard change, nor can it be directly correlated to swings in national opinion on how to manage nature and nature preserves. An examination of Yellowstone's record shows that despite minor changes in the overall popularity of certain elements of the park experience, some basic themes have endured. This permanence is rarely if ever addressed by park scholars, but it is in these long periods of little change—these periods of quiet concern, admiration, and enjoyment of the park—that Yellowstone's spirit evolved.

Electric Peak

THE DISCOVERY ACCOUNTS

Since 1872, much time and effort have been spent searching for "firsts" in Yellowstone. Yellowstone's physical landscape has been combed for evidence of the park's first human inhabitants and first Anglo-European visitors.[1] Even the origins of place-names and road systems have been studied and categorized.[2] Recent scholarship indicates that Native Americans recognized a sense of place unique to the Yellowstone region long before whites entered the surrounding areas.[3] For those interested in the national parks, Yellowstone is revered as the place where the national park idea originated. And its literary landscape has been as laboriously dissected and scrutinized as its physical landscape in the hope of finding evidence documenting the circumstances surrounding the park's creation.[4] However, in their search for heroes and sacred places, these archaeologists of the park's written record have failed to recognize that Yellowstone's value lies not only in its designation as a national park but, perhaps more importantly, in its qualities as place.

Yellowstone's origin as place is distinct from its origin as a national park. The latter can be pinpointed in time: 1 March 1872. Yellowstone's origin as place, however, is less exact. It began with the publication of the "discovery" accounts—the first widely read accounts describing the region that would become Yellowstone National Park—and continued to unfold over several decades. Those who provided the public with its first vicarious views of Yellowstone played a disproportionately large role in determining the evolution of the park's spirit of place, because their words provided the seed from which it would grow.

"DISCOVERERS" AND "DISCOVERY" ACCOUNTS

Rarely are those who first encounter terra incognita honored as its official discoverers. Instead, the title "discoverer" is typically bestowed on those who first communicate new geographic information to others. It is through language—speech, literature, and artistic endeavors—that people make places visible and real, creating places where none previously existed.[5] Such was the case in Yellowstone. The members of three exploratory expeditions are typically credited with discovering the region that became Yellowstone National Park: the Folsom-Cook-Peterson expedition of 1869, the Washburn-Langford-Doane expedition of 1870, and the Hayden Survey of 1871.[6]

But these men were certainly not the first to see Yellowstone. Generations of Native Americans and scores of fur trappers and miners preceded these "discoverers" into the upper reaches of the Yellowstone River. Nevertheless, members of the Folsom, Washburn, and Hayden expeditions are considered by national park scholars to be the park's official discoverers. With their words as much as with their deeds, these explorers "discovered" Yellowstone for the American public and "made particular and important contributions to the emerging popular image of the Yellowstone wonderland."[7] Hence, the park's official discoverers were not the first to see the Yellowstone region but were the first to tell the nation of the region's existence, location, and physical characteristics.

David E. Folsom, Charles W. Cook, and William Peterson, would-be prospectors and fellow ditchdiggers in Helena, Montana Territory, set out on an admittedly impetuous journey into the Yellowstone country in the summer of 1869. Their attempts to publicize the details of their adventures met with little early success. The editors at two periodicals rejected an account written by Cook and Folsom, stating they would not risk their reputations on "such unreliable material."[8] A more sympathetic editor was finally found at the *Western Monthly Magazine* in Chicago.

The following year, General Henry D. Washburn, Nathaniel Pitt Langford (whose initials soon came to stand for National Park Langford), and Lieutenant Gustavus C. Doane of the Second Cavalry led a party of nineteen into Yellowstone. The Washburn party's return resulted in a flurry of newspaper and magazine articles. Langford sent his account of the expedition to *Scribner's Monthly*, assuring him and his portrayal of the expedition an immediate and national audience. He then traveled the country on a lecture circuit sponsored by Jay Cooke of the Northern Pacific Railroad along whose lines the soon-to-be-established park would lie.

After hearing and reading about the Yellowstone region, Professor Ferdinand V. Hayden of the United States Geological and Geographical Survey of the Territories promptly requested funds from Congress to undertake his own official, government-sponsored expedition. He headed west the following year and was lucky enough to have several illustrators in his entourage, two of whom owe the success of their careers to their involvement with the Hayden expedition of 1871. Thomas Moran, who had drawn sketches for Langford's articles published in *Scribner's* the previous year, was one. The

Flashlights illuminate a rare eruption of Steamboat Geyser on September 13, 2002

other artist was William Henry Jackson, a young but very capable and soon-to-be-famous photographer.

Although the park's discoverers wrote or collaborated on a variety of other articles published separately at later dates, the "discovery accounts" referred to here consist of a number of articles and government documents written by members of the 1869, 1870, and 1871 expeditions. These include: Charles Cook and David E. Folsom's "The Valley of the Upper Yellowstone" in the *Western Monthly Magazine* of July 1870; Henry D. Washburn's "The Yellowstone Expedition" in the *Helena Daily Herald* of September 1870 and the *New York Times* and the *Pioneer Press* (St. Paul, Minnesota) of October 1870; Nathaniel P. Langford's "The Wonders of the Yellowstone," Parts One and Two in *Scribner's Monthly* of May and June 1871, respectively; Walter Trumbull's "The Washburn Yellowstone Expedition," Numbers One and Two in *Overland Monthly* of May and June 1871, respectively; Truman Everts's "Thirty-Seven Days of Peril" in *Scribner's Monthly* of November 1871; Gustavus Doane's Senate Executive Document Number 51, 41st Congressional Session of 1871; and Ferdinand V. Hayden's *Preliminary Report of the United States Geological Survey of Montana and Portions of Adjacent Territories* of 1872.

Rather than offering the public seven different views of the newly explored Yellowstone region, the discovery accounts were amazingly alike. Four factors acting separately and in concert helped focus the discoverers' attention on certain aspects of the Yellowstone landscape and narrowed their interpretation and description of it. First, the park's discoverers all had knowledge of "prediscovery" accounts describing Yellowstone. Second, the discoverers set out for the upper reaches of the Yellowstone River at a time of worldwide scientific and geographic exploration. Having read of other expeditions in distant lands, they were aware of their own participation in and contribution to a growing body of exploration literature. Third, Yellowstone's discoverers were greatly influenced by each other. And finally, the discoverers all wrote in the language of their day, obeying linguistic convention and couching their descriptions in familiar terms. Such a writing style made their reports believable, acceptable, and popular with their intended audiences.

PREDISCOVERY ACCOUNTS

As mentioned earlier, the real discovery of the area that became Yellowstone National Park predates its official discovery. More than a handful of accounts describing parts of the Yellowstone landscape, most notably its thermal features, Yellowstone Lake, and the Grand Canyon, were published well before the first of the official discovery expeditions was organized, and many date back to the fur trade era of the 1820s. However, such prediscovery accounts reached only a limited audience and most were considered "tall tales." In local towns and mining camps, rumors had circulated for years about the strange sights, smells, and sounds of the Upper Yellowstone Valley. The inaccessibility of the plateau, however, kept the region secret from the national public who knew little or nothing about the region until reading reports of its official discovery.

Beehive Geyser in eruption

By the 1860s, only bits and pieces of the geographical knowledge accumulated by Rocky Mountain fur trappers and prospectors had found their way into print. Members of all three discovery expeditions described Yellowstone as a terra incognita, yet they repeatedly mentioned finding signs of previous occupation. Members of the Washburn expedition noted in their diaries and published articles that they were probably the first white men ever to view Yellowstone Lake, touting the lake as secluded and pristine and their reaching it a heroic achievement. In almost the same breath, however, these same men told of finding a well-built hunting blind or "rifle-pit" along the lakeshore.[9] In other parts of the park, they reported finding prospect holes and blazed trees, evidence that miners had preceded them. Hayden's *Preliminary Report* of 1872 is full of comments that would lead his readers to believe that Yellowstone was anything but an unknown, uncharted land. In different instances, Hayden wrote, "We followed a well-worn path," or "We were informed by mountain-men that these earthquake shocks are not uncommon," and "The impression among the mountain-men was, that this . . . periodic spring . . . played once in six hours precisely."[10]

More interesting than their comments of finding physical evidence of earlier visitation is the discoverers' specific vocabulary. The particular words, analogies, and phrases chosen by the discoverers suggest that previously written documents were both available to them and deemed credible to them. In writing their own reports, the discoverers borrowed freely from prediscovery accounts written by fur trappers and prospectors. One such trapper was Joe Meek who hunted in the Yellowstone region in the 1830s. In a biography published the year before Hayden led his survey team into the Upper Yellowstone Valley, the trapper was quoted comparing one of Yellowstone's geyser basins to "the City of Pittsburg."[11] In his official report, Hayden described his initial reaction to the geyser basins with, "I can compare the view to nothing but that of some manufacturing city like Pittsburgh."[12] Hence, the discoverers were affected by what they had read prior to their actual arrival in Yellowstone. They came to the park not only with expectations of what they would find but with a well-worn vocabulary to use in communicating their findings to the world.

LANGUAGE OF EXPLORATION

The eighteenth and nineteenth centuries were times of great explorations. From the poles to the abyssal depths of the sea, explorers embarked on religious as well as scientific quests hoping to find evidence of God's plan and purpose for the Earth. A belief in natural theology and the sublime in nature colored the lenses through which explorers viewed their discoveries just as it affected the language of nature writing and the dimensions of landscape art. Members of the Folsom expedition excepted, Yellowstone's discoverers most likely prepared themselves for their journey into Yellowstone's unknown by reading the works of their contemporaries who were actively exploring other parts of the globe. And, they incorporated the language of other discoverers and discoveries into their descriptions.

One important source for both Langford and Hayden was the 1863 work of Dr. Ferdinand Hochstetter on the thermal areas of New Zealand. A decade earlier, Hochstetter had referred to the hot springs at Rotomahana as luxurious bathing pools of "purest marble" with "crystal-clear water."[13] Hochstetter told of pools in which one could choose a bath temperature by sitting in the warmer pools at the top of the spring or cooler pools further from the source. Continuing, Hochstetter wrote, "Immense clouds of steam, reflecting the beautiful blue of the basin . . . present an aspect which no description or illustration is able to represent. It has the appearance of a cataract plunging over natural shelves, which, as it falls, is suddenly turned to stone."[14] Using similar language, Hayden writes of the azure blueness of the water in Yellowstone's Mammoth Hot Springs and suggests they are "bathing-pools . . . arranged one above the other" and "had the appearance of a frozen cascade" or "the appearance of water congealed by frost as it quickly flows down a rocky declivity."[15] Hayden's assistant, A. C. Peale, concurred by stating that "the whole mass looked like some grand cascade that had been suddenly arrested in its descent, and frozen."[16] The following year, Peale repeats a Hochstetter-like description of the Mammoth springs: "The water in all of them is either warm or hot according to their position, the lower ones having the coolest water. The water has also that exquisitely beautiful blue tint which is beyond description, and which forms such handsome contrasts to the white, marble-like basins."[17]

It can be argued that the metaphor of a waterfall may not reflect Hochstetter's influence so much as a valid depiction of reality: the Mammoth Hot Springs terraces do look like frozen waterfalls. Also, the waterfall is a strong and pervasive symbol in the language of the sublime and may have come to mind for that reason as well. However, it cannot be denied that Hayden and Peale's prior reading of Hochstetter's *Neu=Seeland* affected the way they interpreted and described similar thermal features in Yellowstone. Further, by including excerpts from Hochstetter's work in his report to Congress, Hayden gave credibility to his own interpretation of the Mammoth terraces. To a public relatively ignorant of the nature of hot springs, Hayden's description corroborated by Hochstetter's similar description of springs in New Zealand surely must have seemed true and authoritative.

Nathaniel Langford did not see the Mammoth Hot Springs during his discovery expedition of 1870, so his widely distributed and immensely popular articles in *Scribner's* did not mention the terraces. However, when he finally did see the terraces in 1873, he describes them as "congealed cascades, apparently frozen in their descent" and having a whiteness that "exceeds that of purest alabaster."[18] Further evidence of Langford's familiarity with Hochstetter's work appears in his discovery account when Langford writes: "We can only say that the field is open for exploration—illimitable in resource, grand in extent, wonderful in variety, in a climate favored of Heaven, and amid scenery the most stupendous on the continent."[19] This passage is almost a direct translation of Hochstetter's previously published praise for New Zealand as a tourist attraction. Whether consciously or subconsciously, causally or coincidentally, Langford borrowed from Hochstetter while writing his descriptions of Yellowstone.

Fairy Falls

Closer to home, the Yellowstone explorers relied heavily upon each other as sources of information, vocabulary, and inspiration. Members of Hayden's expedition read everything published by the two previous expeditions. Lieutenant Gustavus Doane, leader of the military escort that accompanied the 1870 expedition, published his journal in March of 1871, and Hayden read it in preparation for his own expedition. Hayden praised Doane's work: "For graphic description and thrilling interest, it has not been surpassed by any official report made to our government since the times of Lewis and Clark."[20] The influence of Doane's report on Hayden's subsequent choice of words is obvious. In seeing the bubbling mud pots at Mud Volcano, Doane wrote:

> A Plasterer . . . would go into ecstasies over this mortar, which is worked to such a degree of fineness that it can be dried in large lumps, either in the sun, or in a fire, without a sign of cracking, and when once dry is a soft finely grained stone, resembling clay slate when dark, or meerschaum when white. Mortar might well be good after being constantly worked for perhaps ten thousand years.[21]

The following year, Hayden wrote: "This mud, which has been wrought in these caldrons for perhaps hundreds of years, is so fine and pure that the manufacturer of porcelain-ware would go into ecstasy at the sight. The contents of many of the springs are of such a snowy whiteness that, when dried in cakes in the sun or by a fire, they resemble the finest meerschaum."[22]

It is more difficult to decipher the originator of Doane's descriptions. During most of the 1870 expedition, Doane suffered from a severely infected right thumb, which made keeping his diary up-to-date an impossibility. By the time the swollen digit healed, much of the journey had been completed. In order to catch up on missing journal entries, the lieutenant spent much of his free time copying from Langford's journal into his own. One example of journal copying is found in the similarities in descriptions of Giantess Geyser in eruption. The three expedition leaders—Washburn, Langford, and Doane—shared a common experience that is not likely due purely to chance. Langford wrote that sunlight on the eruptive spray was like "a luminous circle radiant with all the colors of the prism, and resembling the halo of glory represented in paintings as encircling the head of Divinity."[23] Doane wrote that "rainbows encircle the summits of the jets with a halo of celestial glory."[24] Washburn went into more detail but painted essentially the same picture: "Standing and looking down into the steam and vapor of the crater of the Giantess, with the sun upon your back, the shadow is surrounded by a beautiful rainbow, and by getting the proper angle, the rainbow, surrounding only the head, gives that halo so many painters have vainly tried to give in paintings of the Savior."[25] Since Hayden's 1871 party did not see Giantess in eruption, Hayden included Langford's description of Giantess in his report along with Langford's descriptions of Giant and Beehive Geysers taken directly from the *Scribner's* articles.

Hayden borrowed heavily, too, from the Cook-Folsom discovery account, especially in his descriptions of the thermal features. He relied on Cook and Folsom's terms when he pictured the geyserite formations as "beadwork" and "frostwork" and likened the mud pots to bowls of "mush." In different instances, the mud pots reminded Hayden alternately of thick mush, boiling mush, kettles of mush, and caldrons of mush. The mush analogy, however, can be traced back further than Folsom and Cook to a fur trapper named Daniel Potts who wrote to his family of his travels through the Yellowstone region some fifty years earlier. Potts's letter was published without an author in a Philadelphia newspaper in 1827.

Folsom's account reveals that the miner and ditchdigger could write about much more than mush pots and beadwork. David Folsom was well versed in the language of the sublime. In his description of Yellowstone's Grand Canyon published in 1870, Folsom wrote, "we returned to camp realizing, as we have never done before, how utterly insignificant are man's mightiest efforts when compared with the fulfillment of Omnipotent will. Language is entirely inadequate to convey a just conception of the awful grandeur and sublimity of this masterpiece of nature's handiwork."[26] Ferdinand Hayden's writing style proves him to be more than the analytical, unemotional scientist. His *Preliminary Report* of 1872 is a marvelous blend of objective, scientific observation and subjective, descriptive prose strongly influenced by the idea of the sublime. Page after page of all of the discoverers' accounts is filled with elements of the language of the sublime. As described by the discoverers, Yellowstone's almost mythic landscape is beautiful beyond description, the handiwork of God or nature, and far beyond the reach of human artistic endeavors. It inspires religious, intellectual, scientific, patriotic, and artistic contemplation. Yellowstone is dangerous yet fascinating, full of extraordinary and unbelievable features, and all are there for the purpose of amusing, teaching, and inspiring the American public.

Another example of how popular phrases found their way into the Yellowstone record is the appearance and use of the term "freak." The phrases "freak of nature," "freak of the elements," and "freak of Nature's handiwork" are sprinkled liberally throughout the discovery accounts and are used synonymously with "marvel of nature" or "miracle of nature." Almon Gunnison, upon setting out for his journey to Yellowstone with three companions, one of whom was a geology professor from Boston, wrote, "The Professor is elated, for we are going towards wonder-land, and he has absorbing passion for freaks of nature and curious forms of rock and stone."[27] Unlike the language of the sublime, however, the meaning of "freak of nature" has changed over the course of the past century. The customary meaning of the phrase in the late 1800s was that Yellowstone's natural wonders, its freaks, were odd and intriguing. However, in the modern day, by singling out the term "freak" and placing it in quotation marks, some historians would have us believe that Yellowstone was viewed as a modern-day sideshow that aroused a type of curiosity mixed with disgust or fear, distracting tourists from what was really important: the park's natural ecosystems. Interpreted in this way, freak of nature becomes a derogatory term rather than a term of endearment.

Coyote surveys the scene at Mary Bay, Yellowstone Lake

A careful reading of nineteenth-century Yellowstone accounts as well as descriptions of other national parks and newly discovered regions of the American West reveals that the term "freak of nature" was a popular way to describe singularities, not abnormalities. In modern parlance, the word "freak" denotes something bizarre, whereas during the 1800s, a freak was a lighthearted prank or frivolity. "Freak of nature" described the playful, beautiful, unique way nature may express itself. In the Yellowstone literature, the term "freak" was applied to many different conditions and situations. Langford, in his discovery account, described the incrustations around the hot springs as "the most delicate and wonderful freaks of nature's handiwork."[28] And a tourist wrote that nature had painted the Grand Canyon "in a rapturous freak of her mysterious wonder-working."[29] Yellowstone's Isa Lake, thermal features generally, the Devil's Slide, Fishing Cone, and the Wedded Trees were all referred to as freaks. In contrast, however, the marvelous Old Faithful Inn was considered "not in the least a freaky affair."[30] One of the most beautiful examples of how people interpreted the idea of freaks is this description of wildflowers in the mountains of Colorado:

> We find as many strange freaks in the vegetable kingdom here as else-
> where in the Rocky Mountains. Morning after morning in midsummer
> have we shaken the thick, crisp scales of white frost from our blankets,
> and looked sorrowfully around upon a scene of apparent desolation.
> Brilliant flowers of the evening before were a mass of wilted ruins and
> the splendid tall bluegrass, that looked a delicious morsel for stock at
> sunset, was bent and sometimes broken with its weight of a night's
> winter. But an hour of sunshine always changed the scene to one of
> springtime freshness, and often the flora seeming the most delicate
> rallies first under its magic influence.[31]

That tiny flowers could recuperate from what should have been a killing frost truly constituted a freak or unique example of nature's wonders.

The literature of the late 1800s and early 1900s assigned the "freak of nature" label to many features with no hint that it was meant to discount or reduce their affection for the feature. Pikes Peak in Colorado, for example, was described as a place with "peculiar freaks of sculpture and feats of architecture" where even "the clouds were full of freaks that drew forth loud exclamations of wonder and surprise."[32] Yellowstone National Park was indeed set aside because it contained so many marvelous freaks of nature, but to relegate people's feelings to idle curiosity or ogling at a circus sideshow is to do the park a disservice and its patrons a dishonor.

It was a combination of factors that caused the discovery accounts to be more alike than disparate. And, rather than challenging the discoverers' descriptions of Yellowstone with new information and interpretations of the region, subsequent descriptions of the park relied heavily on the information available in the discovery accounts. With few exceptions, authors of Yellowstone articles, books, and guidebooks published in the 1870s and 1880s incorporated the discoverers' descriptions into their own texts. As a result, the words of the discoverers reached an extensive national and international audience and came to cast a broad yet distinct shadow on Yellowstone's evolution as a nationally recognized place.

PUBLICIZING YELLOWSTONE

Immediately following Yellowstone's establishment as "The National Park," a flurry of magazine articles, guidebooks, tourist brochures, and western narratives were published. Most of these consisted primarily of edited versions of the discovery accounts. By the turn of the century, popularizing "The Yellowstone" became a respectable career not only for the discoverers but for those who hoped to build their own reputations as scientists, politicians, or businessmen. These Yellowstone image-builders had strong ties to money, the press, and the federal government, and they put their connections to use in promoting the park and themselves. Railroad companies understood the economic potential of the region and quickly hired writers to sell the park and its environs to tourists and settlers by writing guidebooks and manuals.

In an effort to be first to publish news of Yellowstone and details of the region's unusual features, authors of early guidebooks tended to merely copy passages from the discovery accounts rather than undertake an expensive, difficult, and often dangerous journey to the distant park. A minority of them confessed, apologized, and offered some sort of excuse: "As time did not admit of my visiting these wonders, I present drawings thereof, from original sketches by Mr. Langford's party."[33] Others tried to write as if they had visited the park but betrayed themselves by assigning the wrong names or locations to park features and by copying obviously erroneous information. Robert Strahorn, writer for and employee of the Union Pacific Railroad, told his readers that he found "stone snakes, toads and fishes" along with other petrified items on Yellowstone's Specimen Ridge.[34] Had Strahorn actually climbed Specimen Ridge or been more familiar with his sources, he would quickly have realized the absurdity of his observations.

One of the first guidebooks to appear was James Richardson's 1872 edition of *Wonders of the Yellowstone*, made up entirely of passages from the discovery accounts. The book underwent several editions in the United States and was published in London two years later. A few independent authors contributed to the bank of information from which these and other guidebook authors made withdrawals. H. J. Norton, a resident of nearby Virginia City, Montana, and guidebook author himself, was a favorite source, especially for Strahorn and Henry Winser, an employee of the Northern Pacific Railroad who authored or collaborated on several park guidebooks.

Rossiter W. Raymond toured the park in 1871 and wrote of his experiences in a little book entitled *Camp and Cabin*, and Reverend Edwin Stanley, who published *Rambles in Wonderland* about his travels with wife and daughter in the park in 1873, also added

Grand Canyon of the Yellowstone

greatly to the information available to guidebook authors and editors. By the early 1880s, two other ministers, Reverend Hoyt and Reverend Talmage, were quoted and cited often in Yellowstone books, articles, and travel pamphlets, possibly because it was assumed that their clerical titles gave them—and their impressions of the park—credulity. These two men borrowed heavily from the discovery accounts and used the discoverers' reports as a template for their own writings. Hence, with the exception of Norton's guidebook, much of the material in the early guidebooks came from the discovery accounts. In this way, the image of Yellowstone as perceived and portrayed by the discoverers was rapidly disseminated to a much broader audience than the discovery accounts could reach alone. Sheer repetition strengthened the believability of the image by making it appear that most travelers and travel writers were similarly affected by its landscape.

Because the distance between Yellowstone Park and most of the country's population centers was considerable, would-be tourists made the decision to visit the park well in advance. In addition to distance, a trip to Yellowstone was expensive and dangerous, so tourists familiarized themselves with the region before leaving home. Guidebooks were popular, helpful, and often necessary travel aides. People traveling to the park kept them handy as references during their park tours and often committed much of their contents to memory. Statements such as the following are found throughout the park's published accounts: "The tourist after having metaphorically swallowed half a dozen railroad pamphlets and guides between St. Paul and Livingston, and digested as many descriptions of the Yellowstone National Park . . . should see it as others have described it. He should have all the vocabulary in the front row."[35] Some tourists, unsure of what they would find, hired private guides once they reached the outskirts of the park. One guidebook, hoping to appeal to everyone, went so far as to tout its virtues not only as an ersatz to the expense of a personal guide but to an actual visit to the park. The author insisted that "tourists who use this Book will find it unnecessary to employ Guides. Those who cannot visit the Park will find the Book an excellent substitute."[36] Faith in the veracity and competency of the guidebooks is illustrated in a comment a young tourist made in a letter home to her mother. She wrote, "I can tell you what I have done but I can't describe the things I have seen. I believe I will send you a guide book."[37]

Not all visitors were taken in by their guidebooks' often colorful and persuasive language. In 1883, Margaret Cruikshank, a well-seasoned traveler, made this note in her letters: "In my guidebook, I read that the little pools around [Old] Faithful have 'pink and yellow margins and being constantly wet the colors are "beautiful beyond description."' Then all I can say is that I must be colorblind. . . . I saw none of these."[38] Nor did Ms. Cruikshank believe the distances between park features or the fine quality of the park roads as advertised in her guidebook: "The miles given are, I believe, surveyors' measures, but never were miles so absurdly understated. Be sure of this, that a Park mile according to the book, is worth any two, if not five, elsewhere. . . . Our man, Isaac Door, an experienced Utah state driver said, 'it was a good fifty miles as he ever drove.' Yet the book called it only thirty-six."[39] Other tourists also found fault with their guidebooks.

The following criticism was aimed at H. J. Winser's manual for tourists: "From here onward we rode over a succession of fir clad terraces, 'the charms of which (as the Guide Book says) are apt to cloy.' We found them extremely monotonous, particularly upon a hot day."[40] The passage most likely referred to is from Winser's guidebook wherein he states, "After leaving the falls and the foaming river, the road soon crosses Cañon Creek, passing for the next eight miles over a succession of pine and fir clad terraces, the charms of which are apt to cloy, before the next attractive point is reached."[41]

Rather than undermining the importance of guidebooks in affecting people's expectations of the park experience, these criticisms emphasize their importance. Guidebooks told people what they should see and do, and visitors followed these instructions obediently. "The local guide-books . . . are filled with enticing pictures of existing splendors; and one humbly visits whatever is set down as necessary to be seen," admitted one tourist.[42] "Doing" the Yellowstone quickly became an accepted and standardized tradition: "The horses were sent out to a grassy park a mile up the river, to feast upon the nutritious bunch-grass; and as wood was convenient, and hot and cold water in abundance, we were prepared to 'do' the wonders of Wonderland at our leisure."[43] The repeated behavior of seeing certain sights, participating in certain activities, and experiencing certain emotions eventually manifested the discoverers' image of the Yellowstone experience as reality in the hearts and minds of the public.

Over time, recording the steps in a typical park visit became as important as the trip itself, and a distinct pattern emerges in the park's literary record as people faithfully document their experiences. Naturally, not all tourists had the money, time, or stamina to "do" the park as thoroughly as others. When this was the case, a sort of disclaimer typically appeared in the account followed by an excerpt from a guidebook or other source:

> We could not give time (two days or more) to travel fifty miles farther in order to see the grandest scene of all in this park of wonders—the Grand Cañon. I am told by everyone who has seen it that it is quite impossible by words or paint-brush to give any idea of its grandeur. As, however, any description of the Park which omits the GRAND CAÑON would be like omitting Hamlet from the play, I will give you this quotation from Professor F. V. Hayden's report to Congress.[44]

Other evidence for the pervasive influence of the guidebooks lies in the fact that people repeated the guidebooks' mistakes. There is dogged repetition in Yellowstone accounts of what had to be understood by at least some as misinformation. Tourists would include information in their accounts that seemed unlikely—even preposterous—rather than admit having missed part of the park experience. Evidence of such is found in the persistence of an error in Gustavus Doane's discovery account wherein he described a climb down into Yellowstone's Grand Canyon. In his discovery account, Doane remarked upon the steepness of the canyon walls and the incredible depth of the canyon. After having reached the river, he noted: "looking upward the fearful wall appeared to reach the sky. It was about 3 o'clock p.m., and stars could be distinctly seen; so much of the sunlight was cut off from entering the chasm."[45]

John Richardson included Doane's description of this impossible observation in his 1872 guidebook. The same phenomenon was apparently experienced by General Strong—with only a modicum of restraint—during his 1875 visit to the park. The general noticed that "the vertical walls [of the canyon] are seamed and scarred very strangely, and half-way down they narrow up so that the sunlight is almost excluded."[46] Then, in 1887, in his privately published book of travel in the Yellowstone, Theodore Gerrish, too, experienced the midday darkness: "Should you descend and follow the stream in its tortuous course, you would find many places where the overhanging cliffs seem almost to touch each other two thousand feet above your head; and as you peer up between these rocks, you can see stars in the sky each hour in the day."[47]

In interpreting the evolution of Yellowstone's spirit of place, it is important to recognize both the extent to which bits of early accounts were copied into later accounts and the real impetus or intent behind such copying efforts. For example, in *National Parks: The American Experience*, Alfred Runte suggests that the early national parks—Yellowstone and Yosemite in particular—were not necessarily preserved and protected because of people's affection for "place" or for environmental/ecological concerns; rather it was because these lands were economically useless for purposes such as agriculture and livestock. From a political standpoint, his point is valid and carries much weight. In Yellowstone's case, congressional and other political documents record a strong effort on the part of those wanting to establish Yellowstone as a national park to convince opponents that the region was worthless. Representative Mark H. Dunnell from the Committee on Public Lands, a leader in the crusade to pass the National Park Act, presented the following speech to his fellow congressmen:

> The entire area comprised within the limits of the reservation contemplated in this bill, is not susceptible of cultivation with any degree of certainty, and the winters would be too severe for stock-raising. . . . The mountains are all of volcanic origin, and it is not probable that any mines or minerals of value will ever be found there. . . . There is frost every month of the year.
>
> The withdrawal of this tract, therefore, from sale or settlement takes nothing from the value of the public domain, and is no pecuniary loss to the government, but will be regarded by the entire civilized world as a step of progress and an honor to Congress and the nation.[48]

Dunnell, who had not visited the soon-to-be-established national park himself and who was not an expert on stock raising, farming, or mining, got his information from Ferdinand Hayden directly and from Hayden's discovery account. Dunnell's—read

Hayden's—arguments were then repeated, usually verbatim, by Representative Henry M. Dawes (Massachusetts) and Senators Samuel C. Pomeroy (Kansas) and George F. Edmunds (Vermont) in the House and Senate floor debates. By the time the National Park Act was passed, the worthless lands passage had found its way into most of the National Park Act documents.

But, the "worthless lands" argument was a political construct created to rally support for the Yellowstone bill. It was not the general public's attitude toward the park nor was it the public's justification for removing the Yellowstone region from settlement and occupancy. Many early Yellowstone guidebooks included Dunnell's report to the House pro forma just as they included a copy of the park's enabling act, a list of elevations, average monthly temperatures, and rules and regulations. Hence, people became familiar with the wording of the Dunnell letter just as they became familiar with the discoverers' impressions of park features. The idea of the park as worthless for any purpose other than tourism appears in the historical record not because it is an idea spontaneously generated in the minds of many different people, but because it is a typical inclusion—one of many—that appeared in many park guidebooks and other publications of the time. The public did not need to be convinced of the park's worthlessness to enjoy and appreciate it. One tourist, obviously reciting what he had read, but adding his own observation, wrote, "the Park is of volcanic origin, and therefore devoid of minerals. As the nights are seldom free from frost, farming is an impossibility, *although flowers grow luxuriantly.*"[49] People came to Yellowstone to enjoy the park's scenery, wildness, and tourist facilities, and to be taken in by the spirit of the place. And, people came to Yellowstone prepared to describe the park in a particular way. The typical tourist, after reading the Dunnell letter, may have agreed that Yellowstone was useless for agricultural and other utilitarian purposes, but such thoughts were not necessarily forefront in his or her mind. To the majority of the park's public, Yellowstone was not worthless; it was prized beyond measure.

By the turn of the century, a wide variety of written information about Yellowstone was available to the public. Three railroads boasted that their lines provided the best route to the park. Various stagecoach lines promised luxury service, and tour companies begged for the chance to design people's grand tours of Yellowstone as well as points north, south, east, and west. Each of these concessioners flooded the mail, travel offices, and newsstands with promotional and informative literature. In the early decades of the 1900s, several new guidebooks appeared, such as Hiram Chittenden's definitive *Yellowstone National Park: Historical and Descriptive* and Reau Campbell's *New Revised Complete Guide and Descriptive Book of the Yellowstone.* The *Haynes Guide* became the official park guidebook and, with annual revisions, was published fairly consistently until the 1960s. This guidebook—lavishly filled with photographs by F. J. Haynes, the park's official photographer—eventually swallowed up its competition. However, these new sources of information did little to dilute the strong image of the park already created by the language of the discovery accounts and disseminated through older guidebooks. Many members of the new generation of Yellowstone authors were reluctant to leave

Morning light touches Lower Falls, Grand Canyon of the Yellowstone

behind the language of the now outdated and outmoded discovery accounts. Some clung to the discoverers' words because they best described the incredible impact Yellowstone can have on people who have not yet grown accustomed to stories of its wonders:

> To the early explorers, in particular, who entered this region before it became generally known, its strange phenomena appealed with an imaginative force which the guide-book tourist of to-day can hardly realize. This may account for the fact that some of these explorers, who have never, before or since, put pen to paper with any literary purpose in view, have left in their narratives strokes of word painting which the most gifted writer would find it difficult to excel.[50]

Similarly, other guidebook authors in later years looked back with renewed respect for the discovery accounts and realized the original accounts may have been truly the best description of what the park had come to be: "If quoting from the opinions of others as to the beauties and wonders of the park I seem at this time to prefer those of an earlier day, it is simply because a fresh perusal of their writings profoundly impresses me that they who first penetrated these wilds and saw and wrote, have left a descriptive record that has not been surpassed if, indeed, it has been equalled."[51]

If the Yellowstone region was not a true terra incognita to its discoverers, it was to an eager, impressionable public. After being bombarded with stories and illustrations of the Yellowstone region, people from all over the United States and from foreign countries, young and old, common folk and aristocrats, all joined in a familiar chorus when reciting the wonders of Yellowstone National Park. The word pictures drawn by the discoverers filled their imaginations and created for them a new place, a new geographical reality. Subsequent reports would be written, photographs taken, sketches drawn, and articles published, but the original image of Yellowstone—the one introduced in the discovery accounts—persisted and served as a template for further evolution of the public's perception of the place.

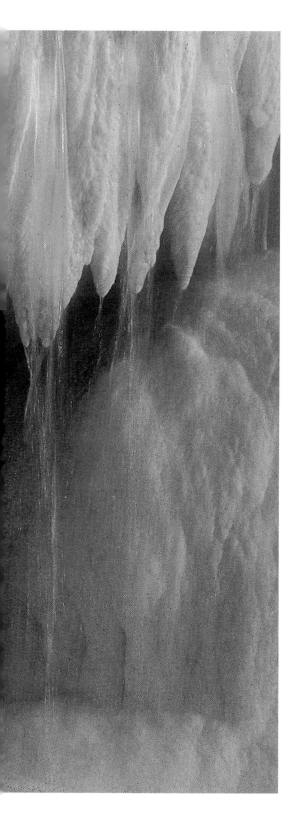
Main Terrace, Mammoth Hot Springs

FOLLOWING IN THE FOOTSTEPS

A handful of Yellowstone's myriad natural wonders stand out in the historical literature: Mammoth Hot Springs, Tower Falls, Old Faithful Geyser and other thermal features, the Grand Canyon of the Yellowstone River, the Upper and Lower Falls, and Yellowstone Lake. Nowadays, these and a few other locations are among the major sight-seeing stops on a typical park tour. The fact that the discoverers chose to describe these particular features attests to their significance in a land full of wonders. Their attraction has not eroded over time.

Ferdinand Hayden's description of the Mammoth Hot Springs terraces is important because neither the Folsom nor the Washburn expedition saw them. Hence, when Hayden notes that the Mammoth springs "had the appearance of a frozen cascade," it was the first description to reach the public and was immediately accepted as definitive. Hayden's frozen cascade analogy appears in most of the early Yellowstone guidebooks and other publications and resurfaces repeatedly in personal accounts as well with no apparent reference to Hayden (or Hochstetter) as the originator.[1]

Geologist Archibald Geikie was most certainly familiar with Hayden's reports. Upon visiting the Mammoth terraces, Geikie wrote, "At many points . . . as one scrambles along that front, the idea of a series of frozen waterfalls rises in the mind."[2] And, frozen cascades appear repeatedly in the poetry of P. W. Norris, one of the early park superintendents. In his poem "Wonderland," Norris mused:

Where the azure pools of healing
Terrace from the snow,
Like a glist'ning cascade frozen,
To the glens below.[3]

Another tourist assigned the phrase to all of the park's thermal features by pointing out that "no one can walk around any of the geysers or hot springs in the park without being reminded of ice-formations which he has seen at waterfalls in winter."[4] The analogy even found its way back into the original German—as "Alabaster versteinerte Kaskade"—in an 1895 article in the *Geographischer Zeitschrift.*[5]

In other parts of his description of the Mammoth terraces, Hayden told of the "wonderful transparency of the water" and the colors of the algae growing in the springs and compared them to "our most brilliant aniline dyes."[6] This passage was so popular, it appeared in guidebooks by Richardson, Stanley, and Strahorn, as did Hayden's description of Mammoth's blue, transparent water that reflected "the sky, with the smallest cloud that flits across it."[7] Lord Dunraven did not cite Hayden as the source of his ideas, but he suggested that "the water is exceedingly clear, clearer than anything I had ever seen before, and of a blue colour, marvellously beautiful to see. The smallest fleck of cloud floating in the sky is reflected in it."[8]

TOWER FALLS

Unlike the Mammoth Hot Springs, Tower Falls was seen by the Washburn-Langford-Doane expedition the year before Hayden reached it, and the influence of the previous year's reports on Hayden's interpretation of the falls is clear. In his discovery account, Langford described the rock formations at the brink of Tower Falls as "towers, others the spires of churches, and others still shoot up as lithe and slender as the minarets of a mosque. Some of the loftiest of these formations, standing like sentinels upon the very brink of the fall, are accessible to an expert and adventurous climber."[9] A year later, Hayden wrote: "on the sides of the gorge the somber pinnacles rise up like Gothic spires . . . standing like gloomy sentinels or like the gigantic pillars at the entrance of some grand temple."[10]

Langford's passage was copied in varying degrees by Brockett, Winser, Riley, and Thayer with and without attribution. In a book entitled *Echoes from the Rocky Mountains*—a book about the West generally rather than Yellowstone specifically—the author, John Clampitt, "echoed" Langford when he wrote that "towers, spires of churches and minarets of mosques rise before you and stand like sentinels upon the brink of the falls."[11]

Lieutenant Doane, too, likened the strangely formed rocks to sentinels, but Doane had a different observation: "Nothing can be more chastely beautiful than this lovely cascade, hidden away in the dim light of overshadowing rocks and woods, its very voice hushed to a low murmur unheard at the distance of a few hundred yards.

Thousands might pass by within a half mile and not dream of its existence, but once seen, it passes to the list of most pleasant memories."[12] This passage was used by Henry Norton and L. P. Brockett and paraphrased in books by Robert Strahorn, William Wylie, W. C. Riley, William Thayer, Hiram Chittenden, and Thomas Murphy. At the Kepler Cascades near Old Faithful, Doane added to his journal: "These pretty little falls if located on an eastern stream would be celebrated in history and song; here amid objects so grand as to strain conception and stagger belief, they were passed without a halt."[13] A combination of these two very similar sentiments found a most interesting expression in tourist accounts. Tourists not only remarked upon the "chaste beauty" of Tower Falls but also on how many of Yellowstone's wonders went unnoticed because of the sheer number of other, more spectacular, curious, and amazing sights. Obviously influenced by Doane, another park visitor wrote of Gibbon Falls that "the falls are not wonderful here, but in New England would be justly famous."[14]

OLD FAITHFUL AND OTHER THERMAL FEATURES

Of all the natural features in the park, the thermal features were the most intriguing to the park's discoverers. Here was something new, unusual, and extraordinary. In the pre-discovery as well as in the discovery accounts, six qualities were repeatedly assigned to travel in the thermal areas: (1) a sense of danger or fear of breaking through the crust and falling into the boiling water below; (2) the eerie sound and sensation of walking on hollow ground; (3) a disagreeable smell, usually sulphur, emanating from the springs or hanging over the basin; (4) a desire to touch the thermal features to verify their existence; (5) a need to retreat to higher and safer ground when surprised by the eruption of either a known geyser or, more typically, an unimpressive feature not thought to possess eruptive behavior; the viewer usually referred to this as having "executed a narrow escape"; and (6) a sense of joy or exhilaration in watching a geyser erupt. Typically, the viewer is physically moved to express himself or herself in some fashion, such as cheering, clapping hands, or throwing hats into the air.

The discoverers' descriptions made lasting impressions on their readers. One of the most popular is Doane's description of Old Faithful Geyser:

> Those who have seen stage representations of Aladdin's Cave and the Home of the Dragon Fly . . . can form an idea of the wonderful coloring, but not of the intricate frost work of this fairy-like yet solid mound of rock growing up amid clouds of steam and showers of boiling water. One instinctively touches the hot ledges with his hands and sounds with a stick the depths of the cavities in the slope, in utter doubt of the evidence of his own eyes. The beauty of the scene takes away one's breath. It is overpowering, transcending the visions of Mosoleum

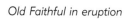
Old Faithful in eruption

[Moslem's] Paradise; the earth affords not its equal, it is the most lovely inanimate object in existence. . . . Rainbows play around the tremendous fountains, the waters which fall about the basin in showers of brilliants, then rush steaming down the slopes to the river.[15]

Doane's description inspired Hayden to write of the "weird beauty" of the geyser, "which wafts one at once into the land of enchantment; all the brilliant feats of fairies and genii in the Arabian Nights' Entertainment are forgotten in the actual presence of such marvelous beauty."[16]

Doane's fanciful description of Old Faithful as a setting for the play about Aladdin's Cave inspired not only Ferdinand Hayden but guidebook authors, and through them, the public. Norton saw "airy phantoms and ogling water-sprites of mythological tales," while Raymond imagined "fairy caverns" inside hot springs and then told how he "half expects to see a lovely naiad emerge with floating grace from her fantastically carved covert."[17]

Langford's descriptions of the thermal features were especially influential since they were accompanied by Thomas Moran's sketches—drawn sight unseen—from Langford's descriptions and no small dose of Moran's own imagination.[18] Langford's geyser descriptions had such an impact on Ferdinand Hayden that he copied many of them into his official report. In the case of Giantess Geyser, Hayden confessed that since "it has been so graphically described by Mr. Langford, and so faithfully depicted by Mr. Moran, the artist, that little more need be added." Hayden assumed the public was already well acquainted with Langford's descriptions: "If I should here describe the Giant, Grotto, Punch-Bowl, and a hundred other geysers of all classes, it would be pretty much a repetition of what has already been written."[19]

Some guidebook authors used Langford's or Doane's description of Giantess (the two are very similar) to describe not only Giantess but other geysers in eruption. Possibly because Doane also described Giantess as "the grandest . . . fountain in the world," Robert Strahorn mistakenly assigned Doane's description of Giantess to Grand Geyser in his 1881 guidebook,

"In the Geyser Basin" from Stanley's Rambles in Wonderland *(1880). The illustrator shows simultaneous eruptions of several major geysers in the Upper Geyser Basin.*

IN THE GEYSER BASIN.

52

*"Simultaneous Eruptions"
sketch from Riley's Official
Guide to Yellowstone National
Park (1889)*

copying Doane's entire Giantess passage and passing it off as his own description of Grand. The same copying mistake appeared in Brockett and Thayer.[20]

Not only were the geysers' physical appearances described in the discovery accounts but details of their behavior were included as well. The propensity to "salute" was one such common remark. Langford wrote that he and his party were saluted by the geysers in the Upper Geyser Basin, as did Captain Barlow: "As we were leaving the valley 'Old Faithful' gave us a splendid display by way of a parting salute."[21] Later, Colonel John Gibbon wrote: "As though we were not to be permitted to leave this enchanting region without seeing it in the very height of its splendor, it is a remarkable fact that, as we moved along, each geyser, as we passed, broke out in succession, as if giving us a parting salute."[22]

It is unlikely that Gibbon actually saw all the geysers in the Upper Basin erupt or salute at once. In the winter of 1887, Frank J. Haynes witnessed and photographed a simultaneous eruption of Old Faithful, Grand, Giantess, and Castle Geysers. And, on the night of the 1959 Hebgen Lake earthquake, almost all of the thermal features in the Upper Geyser Basin erupted to some degree. However, these were rare occurrences and it is doubtful that park visitors really saw all the simultaneous eruptions they report seeing. Nevertheless, from the reports of geyser activity in guidebooks and from the accompanying illustrations, early tourists could easily conclude that such geyser activity was the norm. As with other mistakes faithfully transcribed into personal accounts, tourists dutifully documented seeing many geysers erupt at once and included illustrations of the same. In a passage typical of railroad promotional literature describing the park in anthropomorphic terms—making it seem tame, civilized, and therefore not dangerous—Olin Wheeler, spokesman for the Northern Pacific line, wrote: "From afar Old Faithful espied me, and, recognizing an old friend, trumpeted a salute in his hearty, royal fashion, welcoming me again to his presence. Within fifteen minutes the Bee Hive, not to be outdone in hospitality, did the same, and altogether I felt that I had a *warm* welcome."[23]

In general, guidebook authors incorporated a variety of the discoverers' impressions of the geysers and thermal regions into their own accounts, assigning certain characteristics to different features or certain experiences to different places. Just as the discoverers immortalized Old Faithful's punctuality with its name, so they endowed Giantess Geyser with a feminine beauty and a share of the power they associated with her spouse, Giant

Moonset over Lower Falls, Grand Canyon of the Yellowstone

Geyser. Giving human qualities to the geysers and other thermal features was common practice. Geysers typically "groaned" or "bellowed" prior to the "spasms" of an eruption caused by the feature's "passion," "fury," or "suffering." One guidebook author informed his readers that "there is much individuality found in the geyser family." In fact, "some of them are wonderfully lazy, others have a surplus of energy. The smaller tots and babies are like human children, full of antics. They are impressible, and, like many a young hopeful, 'show off' when least expected, are quiet when it is desired that they exhibit their accomplishments."[24]

Another important aspect of the geyser basins was the dangerous footing and the need for caution and vigilance: "A horseman recently rode too near one of the pools, and the animal, in his terror, broke the crust, releasing a column of sulphur vapor which was almost overpowering. The escape of horse and rider from a horrible death was very narrow."[25] In a letter home to her children, a wife and mother explained that their father "came pretty near getting a good scald as he peered into the throat of 'Old Faithful,'" and she herself "tripped rather lively over the geyserite surface and pools, lest the boiling water should overtake" her.[26] Geyser basins *are* dangerous places and many of the close calls described undoubtedly occurred. But the fact that so many people chose to include descriptions of such narrowly averted disasters and always with the same terminology is a good indication of how deeply they were influenced by the substance of the discovery accounts.

On a brighter and often more humorous note, many tourists delighted in telling of how they used the hot springs for washing dishes:

> We are told of a tourist who washed the dishes, his first attempt probably in a lifetime. . . . Pitching the soiled tinware, knives, forks, towels, etc., into a champagne basket . . . unceremoniously dumped them in to soak while he placidly enjoyed his meerschaum. Suddenly, and as if resenting the insult to its dignity, the little spouter spit the basin full to overflowing in a second, setting the contents in a perfect whirl, and the next instant, drawing in its breath, commenced sucking everything toward the aperture. Others at the camp heard an agonizing cry for help, and looking out, beheld the watcher, with hat off and eyes peeled, dancing around his dish pan in a frantic attempt to save the fast disappearing culinary outfit. . . . There would be a plunge of the hand in the boiling water, a yell of pain, and out would come a spoon; another plunge and yell, and a tin plate; and "Oh! ah! o-o-o!—e-e-e!" and a fork, etc.[27]

Robert Strahorn copied this story verbatim from Norton's 1873 guidebook, and the idea soon became a popular one. It was not long before washing dishes and then washing clothes in the thermal features was a favorite housekeeping chore associated with a trip to Yellowstone. Eventually, laundering instructions were included as well: "Soiled linen

Sunrise on the Grand Canyon of the Yellowstone River

placed in the crater is thoroughly cleansed and uninjured in the process; woolens are, however, destroyed.[28] Those who repeated these instructions were probably referring to a story that surfaced originally in a Robert Strahorn publication, although Strahorn most likely got the story from Norton. An oft-repeated version of this particular story appeared in a book written by Carrie Strahorn, Robert's wife, who accompanied her husband on his transcontinental journey along the line of the Union Pacific Railroad. The story as told by Carrie follows:

> Near one of the small laundry geysers sat a workman who had been haying in a meadow close by, and whose facial expression betokened deep trouble. After some questioning he said the boys told him that if he put his woollen shirt in the geyser when it was getting ready to spout that the cleansing waters would wash it perfectly clean while it whipped it in the air. He had followed their advice and twisting a piece of flannel about three inches square in his finger, he said that was all he could find of his shirt when the waters got quiet, and he said he guessed it had gone down to H—— to be ironed, and he marched off declaring he would "lick them fellers" if they would not buy him a new shirt.[29]

By the time the National Park Service was formed in 1916, washing, cooking, and tossing things in the thermal features were prohibited—as was the generally deplorable prank of writing one's name in the hot pools surrounding geyser formations. However, stories telling of such activities persist in the park literature, although usually attributed to other people's doings at some past date.

GRAND CANYON OF THE YELLOWSTONE RIVER

The discoverers' descriptions of the Grand Canyon of the Yellowstone River are classic examples of nature writing of the romantic period. They are full of allusions to the sublime in nature, and descriptions of Yellowstone's Grand Canyon have much in common with descriptions of the Grand Canyon in Arizona and the waterfalls and valleys of Yosemite Park written during the same era. Langford's popular description of Yellowstone's Grand Canyon follows:

> The brain reels as we gaze into this profound and solemn solitude. We shrink from the dizzy verge appalled, glad to feel the solid earth under our feet . . . The stillness is horrible. Down, down, down, we see the river attenuated to a thread, tossing its miniature waves, and dashing, with puny strength, the massive walls which imprison it. All access to its margin is denied, and the dark gray rocks hold it in dismal shadow. Even the voice of its waters in their convulsive agony cannot be

heard. Uncheered by plant or shrub, obstructed with massive boulders and by jettying points, it rushes madly on its solitary course, deeper and deeper in to the bowels of the rocky firmament. The solemn grandeur of the scene surpasses description. It must be seen to be felt. The sense of danger with which it impresses you is harrowing in the extreme. You feel the absence of sound, the oppression of absolute silence.[30]

Apparently, Langford's initial experience at the canyon was not unmitigated joy and deep appreciation for the beauty of the scene. Instead, Langford emphasized—perhaps overemphasized—the painful silence and sense of danger that accompanied peering into the abyss. Oftentimes, it is not Langford's vocabulary so much as the sensations he associated with the canyon that make his description the basis for others' writings. Riley wrote that "the view altogether is weird and appalling, while the profound solitude and absolute silence impress the beholder with an overwhelming sense of his own insignificance."[31] The Reverend Mr. Hoyt must have been familiar with Langford's discovery account when he composed the following: "Nothing more awful have I ever seen than the yawning of that chasm. And the stillness, solemn as midnight, profound as death! The water dashing there as in a kind of agony against those rocks, you cannot hear. The mighty distance lays the finger of its silence on its white lips. You are oppressed with a sense of danger . . . The silence, the sheer depth, the gloom burden you."[32] Written in 1878, Hoyt's account first appeared in the nationally circulated literature in 1881 and

"Stalactitic Basins" (Mammoth Hot Springs), photograph by William Henry Jackson from Ferdinand Hayden's Twelfth Annual Report.

quickly became an important addition to the various guidebooks. The passage above is either quoted verbatim or paraphrased in many guidebooks published during the 1880s and appeared in the *Haynes Guides* until the 1930s.

If Langford's accounts related the size and depth of the canyon to his readers, then Hayden's account attested equally to its color and form:

> But no language can do justice to the wonderful grandeur and beauty of the cañon below the Lower Falls . . . the river appears like a thread of silver foaming over its rocky bottom; the variegated colors of the sides, yellow, red, brown, white, all intermixed and

shading into each other; the Gothic columns of every form standing out from the sides of the walls with greater variety and more striking colors than ever adorned a work of human art. . . . Mr. Thomas Moran, a celebrated artist, and noted for his skill as a colorist, exclaimed with a kind of regretful enthusiasm that these beautiful tints were beyond the reach of human art.[33]

Reverend Hoyt expanded on Hayden's attention to color:

> The whole gorge flames. It is as though rainbows had fallen out of the sky and hung themselves there like glorious banners. The underlying color is the clearest yellow; this flushes onward into orange. Down at the base the deepest mosses unroll their draperies of the most vivid green; browns, sweet and soft, do their blending; white rocks stand spectral; turrets of rock shoot up as crimson as though they were drenched through with blood. It is a wilderness of color. It is impossible that even the pencil of an artist tell it. . . . It is as though the most glorious sunset you ever saw had been caught and held upon that resplendent, awful gorge![34]

Reverend Talmage, not to be outdone by a fellow man of the cloth, wrote that the canyon has "triumphant banners of color . . . Sunrise and Sunset married by the setting of a rainbow ring" and then went on in unbelievable prose: "Formations of stone in shape and color of calla-lily, of heliotrope, of rose, of cowslip, of sunflower, and of gladiola. . . . Wide reaches of stone of intermingled colors—blue as the sky, green as the foliage, crimson as the dahlia, white as the snow, spotted as the leopard, tawny as the lion, grizzly as the bear—in circles, in angles, in stars, in coronets, in stalactites, in stalagmites."[35] Elia Peattie, author of the pamphlet in which Talmage is quoted, concluded his section on the Grand Canyon with, "After this it seems superfluous for me to mention anything I saw or thought in this wonderful country."[36] The public must have accepted such hyperbole, because Hoyt and Talmage's accounts appear almost as often as the discoverers' own words in later guidebooks.

At the Grand Canyon of the Yellowstone, the typical Yellowstone tourist wrote of experiencing many of these same emotions and sensations. Individual tourists told of the canyon's dizzying depth and a feeling of speechlessness, timelessness, and insignificance in the face of God or nature. The painful silence first recorded by Langford was commonly referred to, although in later years, the solemn and terrible silence changed to a reverent hush. Statements such as, "We were awed into silence and reverence . . . and we almost felt that we were trespassing on sacred ground" were common.[37] Rudyard Kipling noted that after viewing the canyon, "The maid from New Hampshire said no word for a very long time. She then quoted poetry, which was perhaps the best thing she could have done."[38]

The Yellowstone record shows that viewing the Canyon was often a moving, spiritual experience. And, since mere words often failed to adequately convey the impact of the scene, individuals turned to other means of expression: "The long meter doxology was sung at Inspiration Point, the only thing that would in part express what we feel."[39] Reciting poetry or Scripture, singing hymns, and capturing the beauty on paper or canvas are offered as attempts to give voice to some idea of the beauty, color, size, and form of the landscape:

> My daughter endeavored to produce a water color sketch that would afford some idea, at least, of the colors; but she found that every stone and rock required to be painted separately, while the hues were altering with each change of light, and after working faithfully all the forenoon she gave up in despair, and said it would require a month to reproduce the scene, even roughly. She consoled herself, however, for this disappointment by executing a little waltz upon the little rocky platform from which she had been sketching, and which projected over the depths of the Cañon, to the speechless horror of her mother.[40]

Regardless of how they accomplished the task, tourists felt the need to express to others the idea that they had been moved—spiritually, emotionally, even physically (some to tears)—by the sheer beauty of the landscape. For many people, experiencing Yellowstone's Grand Canyon was more than an exercise in tourism. It truly was an experience of the sublime.

THE UPPER AND LOWER FALLS

On the Yellowstone River at the head of the Grand Canyon are two large waterfalls. The Upper Falls, over 100 feet high, is so named because it lies upstream. The Lower Falls, nearly three times higher, is just downstream, hence, "lower" on the river. Each of the discoverers not only described the two waterfalls individually but compared the waterfalls to each other and to the surrounding canyon. Langford began this practice by comparing the waterfalls to the canyon:

> The life and sound of the cataract, with its sparkling spray and fleecy foam, contrasts strangely with the sombre stillness of the cañon a mile below. There all was darkness, gloom, and shadow; here all was vivacity, gayety, and delight. One was the most unsocial, the other the most social scene in nature. We could talk, and sing, and whoop, waking the echoes with our mirth and laughter in the presence of the falls, but we could not thus profane the silence of the cañon.[41]

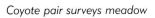
Coyote pair surveys meadow

Later in this same account, he pointed out that the "upper fall is entirely unlike the other." What the Upper Falls "lacks in sublimity is more than compensated by picturesqueness."[42] Doane's descriptions of the two waterfalls were less dramatic than Langford's, but in an interesting passage, Doane added:

> Both of these cataracts deserve to be ranked among the great waterfalls of the continent. No adequate standard of comparison between such objects, either in beauty or grandeur, can well be obtained. Every great cascade has a language and an idea peculiarly its own, embodied, as it were, in the flow of its waters. Thus the impression on the mind conveyed by Niagara may be summed up as "Overwhelming power"; of the Yosemite, as "Altitude"; of the Shoshone Fall, in the midst of a desert, as "Going to waste." So the upper fall of the Yellowstone may be said to embody the idea of "Momentum," and the lower fall of "Gravitation." In scenic beauty, the upper cataract far excels the lower. It has life, animation, while the lower one simply follows its channel; both, however, are eclipsed, as it were, by the singular wonders of the mighty cañon below.[43]

The following year, it was noted that the Upper Falls was the "embodiment of beauty," and the Lower Falls was "that of grandeur."[44] Lord Dunraven characterized the Upper Falls as Langford did, "being more instinct with life, motion, and variety than the other," which is "by far the most impressive."[45] Winser concurred and stated that the Upper Falls "is full of life and action, possessing a beauty peculiar to itself."[46] Winser's description was then copied in Riley's guidebook, and later, in his pamphlets for the Northern Pacific Railroad, Olin Wheeler continued the tradition:

> I confess that to me the upper fall was the greater attraction. There is beyond question a superb spectacle, superiority of power, the effect of crushing, irresistible force, and withal, a stately, noble dignity in the lower fall that compels the homage of the beholder. But there is in the upper fall a life, action, vivacity, energy that are simply irresistible . . . . Rampant with animation and joy, it represents the tireless activity and energy of youth, while the greater cataract typifies the more mature and sedate manhood.[47]

"Grand Cañon of the Yellowstone," chromolithograph by Thomas Moran for Ferdinand Hayden's Twelfth Annual Report. *No such vantage point really exists, although a lookout on the South Rim of the Canyon is named Artist Point, supposedly because Moran painted different versions of this scene from that particular location.*

Bull elk guards his harem as the sun rises at Yellowstone Lake

YELLOWSTONE LAKE

Upstream from the falls and Grand Canyon lies Yellowstone Lake. One of the most popular descriptions of Yellowstone Lake first appeared in Charles Cook and David Folsom's 1869 discovery account:

> Nestled among forest-crowned hills which bounded our vision, lay this inland sea, its crystal waves dancing and sparkling in the sunlight as if laughing with joy for their wild freedom. It is a scene of transcendent beauty which has been viewed by few white men, and we felt glad to have looked upon it before its primeval solitude should be broken by the pleasure seekers which at no distant day will throng its shores.[48]

This description of the lake as secluded and pristine appeared in almost all early guidebooks, and Folsom and Cook's original description continued to be cited in annual editions of the *Haynes Guide* until 1947. As pictured in these materials, Yellowstone Lake seemed "civilized and habitable, and is a most restful place after the tour in the infernal regions."[49] At Yellowstone Lake Hotel, tourists could stop a while and engage in the more usual vacation activities: "Among the Park hotels this is the one the tourist will probably choose if he wishes to remain a few days and rest. Here he can fish, row a boat, go out to the Natural Bridge, lounge among the trees, watch the bears at night . . . or enjoy the splendid view."[50]

All of the discoverers were taken in by the beauty of the lake, "a vast sheet of quiet water, of a most delicate ultramarine hue,"[51] and they rarely failed to point out its shape, which they likened to the human hand. More intriguing still were the hot springs along the lakeshore where fish caught in the lake could be cooked. The discoverers warned their readers, however, that trout caught in the lake were usually "wormy." Rossiter Raymond added a bit of humor concerning this latter point when he commented on the ease of catching trout in the lake: "The wormy fellows bit the best, which is strange, when one considers that they have already more bait in them than is wholesome."[52]

HISTORICAL CONTINGENCY AND CHANCE

The events and circumstances that led to the publication of the discovery accounts—the incredible stories told by fur trappers and miners, the collaboration of scientists and explorers, the popularity of the language of the sublime, and the sharing of journals—were a matter of chance. It could not have been predicted that David Folsom, Charles Cook, and William Peterson would trek into the upper Yellowstone River valley in order to verify tall tales or that others would read their journals before undertaking similar expeditions. Similarly, who could have guessed that Gustavus Doane would injure his thumb, requiring him to copy "National Park" Langford's journal entries? As a result, however, a sharply focused image of the Yellowstone region was presented to the public

Sunset sky near Yellowstone Lake

simultaneously with word of its discovery, and a clearly defined "Yellowstone!" erupted onto the American consciousness. The subsequent formation of Yellowstone as place and the establishment of Yellowstone as a national park were not random events. They were the result of a series of linked events inexorably tied to this place at that time.

The peculiar characteristics of the discovery accounts both opened up opportunities and formed constraints that would steer the course of Yellowstone's transformation from a blank spot on the map into Yellowstone National Park. Yellowstone's emergence as place, however, is distinct from Yellowstone's origin as the first national park. The true origins of the national park idea, like the true origin or discovery of the Yellowstone, may never be known. Time has most likely obscured direct evidence pinpointing the inception of the national park idea and the true discovery of the region that was to become Yellowstone National Park. It may be, however, that these events have no distinct origins. Stephen Jay Gould suggests that people are generally uncomfortable with evolutionary modes of explanation because "evolutionary stories provide no palpable, particular thing as a symbol for reverence, worship, or patriotism."[53] Yet Yellowstone—despite its hazy origins—has become a place of shared affection, reverence, and patriotism, and it was the discovery accounts that were both the vocabulary and the vehicle of this transformation.

Sunset over the Lower Geyser Basin

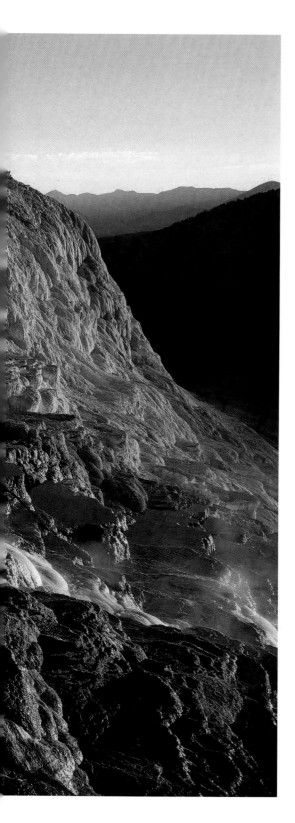

Main Terrace, Mammoth Hot Springs

THE ART OF THE YELLOWSTONE

By the turn of the century, Yellowstone became a recognized place with traditions familiar to most Americans. The elements of a typical Yellowstone experience found their way into textbooks, scientific articles, government reports, children's literature, and fictional works. Ernest Thompson-Seton's stories of Waub the bear; Herbert Quick's romantic fiction, *Yellowstone Nights*; and Andrew Lincoln's adventure, *Motorcycle Chums in Yellowstone Park*, are all set in Yellowstone and incorporate the park's real or invented natural features into their story lines. These books and later movies perpetuated the discoverers' initial image of the park. However, it was not only the discovery accounts that made a lasting impression. The illustrations that accompanied them were copied, embellished or rearranged, and authenticated over time through republication as well.

In the United States of the late 1800s, artists began painting huge canvases depicting the vast, wild, and beautiful landscapes beyond the Missouri River, and Thomas Moran was one of these "new age" artists. Moran was a young, unknown artist when he was hired by *Scribner's Monthly* magazine to illustrate Langford's discovery accounts. Since he had not yet seen the Yellowstone region for himself, Moran drew his sketches based on Langford's descriptions alone. This work so fascinated him, however, that he joined the Hayden expedition at his own expense the next summer to see Yellowstone with his own eyes. As one of Moran's biographers pointed out, Moran found that in Yellowstone, "actuality . . . was even more bizarre" than some of his imaginative drawings.[1]

Thomas Moran's sketch of Devil's Slide for Langford's Scribner's Monthly *in 1871 before Moran saw the feature*

These early *Scribner's* illustrations were highly romanticized, more a product of adherence to Langford's exaggerated and romantic descriptions as well as ideas about the sublime than of reality. Moran's drawing of Devil's Slide is a good example. Of this geologic feature, Langford wrote:

> The sides are as even as if they had been worked by line and plumb— the whole space between, and on either side of them, having been completely eroded and washed way. We had seen many of the capricious works wrought by erosion upon the friable rocks of Montana, but never before upon so majestic a scale. Here an entire mountainside, by wind and water, had been removed, leaving as the evidences of their protracted toil these vertical projections, which, but for their immensity, might as readily be mistaken for works of art as of nature. . . . In future years, when the wonders of the Yellowstone are incorporated into the family of fashionable resorts, there will be few of its attractions surpassing in interest this marvelous freak of the elements.[2]

The Devil's Slide near the north entrance. Photo by Judith L. Meyer

As drawn by Moran, there are two symmetrical "handrails" on either side of the Slide, and the feature is situated in a mountainous landscape. The "symmetry of nature" as an expression of God's perfection is a common theme underlying the art and literature of the Romantic Movement. "Mountains as sublime," too, falls into this

*Thomas Moran's sketch of
Grotto Geyser for Langford's
Scribner's Monthly article*

understanding of natural landscapes being God's handiwork: perfect, overwhelming, and ominous. Moran incorporated both these elements in his depiction of Devil's Slide, despite the fact that the Slide is neither symmetrical nor located in the mountains.

Moran's first depiction of Grotto Geyser was similarly fanciful. But, based on Langford's description, it provided *Scribner's* readers with their first visual evidence of Yellowstone's wonders. Langford wrote,

> The Grotto was so named from its singular crater of vitrified sinter, full of large, sinuous apertures. Through one of these, on our first visit, one of our company crawled to the discharging orifice; and when, a few hours afterwards, he saw a volume of boiling water, four feet in diameter, shooting through it to the height of sixty feet, and a scalding stream of two hundred inches flowing from the aperture he had entered a short time before, he concluded he had narrowly escaped being summarily cooked.[3]

Another of Moran's *Scribner's* illustrations revealed Moran's reliance on a source other than Langford's descriptions. Although not included in the originally published versions of the discovery accounts, illustrations of some Yellowstone features were drawn by Washburn-Langford-Doane expedition members Walter Trumbull and Private Moore. These two men must have made their drawings available to Langford and Moran, since Moran's 1871 "Castle Geyser" was almost identical to an earlier sketch by Trumbull and Moore. Langford's brief description of the geyser—"'The Castle' . . . has a turreted crater"[4]—was too vague to prompt a drawing with such detailed similarities. Few readers, however, were aware that Moran drew not from experience but from Langford's text,

CASTLE GEYSER CONE.
ORIGINAL SKETCH.

Drawing of Castle Geyser by Walter Trumbull and Private Moore of the Washburn-Langford-Doane expedition of 1870, but not published until 1905 when Langford included it in the appendix of his book, The Discovery of Yellowstone Park

Thomas Moran's Castle Geyser from Langford's 1871 Scribner's Monthly article

and Moran's sketches gave credence to Langford's word painting. When tourists later saw for themselves the features Moran had drawn, they agreed that Langford's descriptions were accurate.

Moran's later works were a bit more realistic, and Moran was a major illustrator for Hayden's official government reports. Moran's painting of the Grand Canyon and Falls of the Yellowstone River, completed after traveling to the park with the Hayden expedition of 1871, was one of his greatest, most popular works. Park visitors commonly referred to it and were eager to travel to the park so they could compare the painting with the real thing. Prior to a trip to the park, one tourist mentioned that for him and his traveling companions, "the pictures of Moran have made us impatient to see the wonders of the Yellowstone."[5] Typically, such remarks fell into two categories. Either they repeated Hayden's well-publicized statement that even Moran himself, "a celebrated artist, and noted for his skill as a colorist, exclaimed with a kind of regretful enthusiasm that these beautiful tints were beyond the reach of human art"[6] or tourists chastised themselves for not believing Moran's depiction. Almost a century later, William Henry Jackson praised Moran's work by stating: "So far as I am concerned, the great picture of the 1871 expedition was no photograph, but a painting by Moran of Yellowstone Falls."[7] W. H. Jackson knew whereof he spoke. He, too, was a Yellowstone artist. Hayden used Jackson's photographs liberally in his government reports, especially the annual report of 1883. Hayden felt that the visual evidence provided by Jackson's photographs would substantiate his interpretation of the landscape, since photographs were considered a more objective representation of reality than sketches and paintings. William Henry Holmes accompanied the Hayden Surveys of 1872 and 1878 primarily as a geologist but also as

William Henry Jackson's photograph of Grotto Geyser from Hayden's Twelfth Annual Report

an illustrator. Holmes's sketches filled the pages of Hayden's later Yellowstone reports and were used extensively by guidebook and other authors as the basis for their own illustrations.

During the park's first decade and long before the invention of portable cameras,

Grotto Geyser (near right) from John Gibson's Great Waterfalls, Cataracts, and Geysers (1887). The perspective is such that the lone human figure shrinks in size relative to the geyser. Gibson's illustrator probably used W. H. Jackson's photograph of Grotto Geyser as a template for his own drawing (see photo above).

Grotto Geyser (far right) from F. K. Warren's California Illustrated (1892). In this sketch, the geyser itself does not monopolize the scene so much as provide a backdrop for the human figures approaching it. However, the geyser is still portrayed much too large relative to the size of the people. The drawing of the geyser is basically the same as in Gibson's work of five years previously (photo near right), but more people have been added to the scene.

there was a dearth of pictures of Yellowstone. Hence, most early park illustrations found in popular magazines and books were either exact or modified copies of the original works by Moran, Jackson, and Holmes. A single picture might be reproduced for a variety of publications with only slight modification depending on the purpose or intended audience. For example, in

Sketch of explorers surveying the Mammoth Hot Springs from Ferdinand Hayden's Twelfth Annual Report

the book *Great Waterfalls, Cataracts, and Geysers,* Grotto Geyser is drawn unrealistically large, dominating the landscape.[8] The illustrator probably copied Grotto Geyser from Jackson's photograph and then added human figures. The people are disproportionately small, however, exaggerating the size of the geyser in comparison. This doctored image of Grotto Geyser became the template for illustrations in other books, including Warren and Butterworth who added even more human figures engaged in various tourist activities.[9]

In another example, an early drawing of Mammoth Hot Springs depicting members of the Hayden expedition surveying the sights was used as the basis for an illustration in a book published well after a hotel, roads, and other tourist amenities had been constructed at Mammoth. The explorers in the original drawing were joined in the later drawing

A later sketch of tourists at Mammoth Hot Springs from J. C. Fennell's article in The California Illustrated Magazine *of 1892. The explorers are still present but have faded into the background.*

This illustration from Hezekiah Butterworth's Zigzag Journeys (circa 1892) consists of yet another scantily clad human figure next to a hot spring formation similar to the photo below but with the addition of another, more realistic view of the terraces in the background. Exactly the same sketch is found in F. K. Warren's California Illustrated.

"Ornamental Basins at Mammoth Hot Springs of Gardiner's River" from F. V. Hayden's Twelfth Annual Report. The abstract hot spring fountain and the mythical figure may have been included because characters from Greek and Roman mythology were often used in naming natural features. Various springs at Mammoth had already been named Jupiter, Minerva, and Cleopatra.

by smartly dressed, genteel tourists, giving the impression that the park had changed to a modern, civilized tourist resort. In a 1903 *Century* magazine article written by Pulitzer Prize–winning Ray Stannard Baker and illustrated by Ernest L. Blumenschein, cartoon-like caricatures of tourists were added to an otherwise realistic scene of the Mammoth terraces.

In the park's early years, book and magazine publishers faced a paucity of authentic illustrations depicting park features as well as a general lack of knowledge about the park. Some authors and editors betrayed their ignorance by including incorrectly labeled illustrations. For example, F. K. Warren's *California Illustrated* contained three different illustrations of Giant Geyser, each time with a different name, and in unrelated portions of the chapter. The first Giant Geyser illustration was taken from an 1880 book by Stanley and had a "The Giant Geyser" label. Four pages later, the drawing Moran made for Langford's *Scribner's* (but

"Mud Volcanoes" from F. K. Warren's California Illustrated *(1890)*

Crater of the Giant Geyser as Moran sketched it for Langford's Scribner's *article in 1870*

drawn with help from Moore and Trumbull's sketch) appeared with the caption "Mud Volcanoes." Finally, an illustration of Giant taken from Hayden's *Twelfth Annual Report* and labeled "Giant Geyser in Action" in the original appeared in Warren's book labeled "A Sudden Eruption." The fact that Warren used three views of the same geyser with different captions indicates he either failed to recognize they were all different views of the same geyser or he had only a small number of geyser illustrations from which to choose.

Some authors and illustrators added to the Yellowstone mystique by designing their own compositions from illustrations that were poorly or incorrectly drawn from the start. One picture in Hayden's *Annual Report* of 1878 showed an imaginary figure standing at a highly abstracted Mammoth Hot Springs. More than a decade later, the illustrator for Butterworth and Warren redesigned this original sketch, added another view of the terraces in the background, and included it in both their books.

The early art of the Yellowstone—the sketches, photographs, and chromolithographs that accompanied the discovery accounts—were as important in creating the public's image of Yellowstone as "place" as was the language of the discovery accounts. Both were incorporated into subsequent Yellowstone publications and quickly diffused through newspapers, magazines, travel brochures, and books into homes, libraries, and

"A Sudden Eruption" from F. K. Warren's California Illustrated *(1890)*

A SUDDEN ERUPTION.

travel offices across the nation and into Europe. The American public was willing to believe almost anything about Yellowstone that was set before it in print—especially if written by distinguished scientists and explorers, corroborated in the popular press, and confirmed by accompanying sketches, paintings, and photographs. From its inception, the park's initial image was vivid, colorful, and detailed. Through repetition and wide dissemination, elements of the discovery accounts eventually became real, enduring for generations, modified rather than replaced by time.

People have always come—and probably always will come—to Yellowstone pre-programmed to encounter, interpret, and describe the park in particular ways. However, such expectations do not preclude fascination and surprise. Even today, when so much has been written, painted, and photographed, tourists still find something about the Yellowstone that is a surprise: "There is in all of us a need to wonder, to discover, and Yellowstone has more than its share of such moments. Each time an animal shows, or a geyser erupts, or the sun shines in a particular way. Each is new and now and gone. No wonder we try to lock these moments away in our hearts."[10] In Yellowstone, "it cannot be said that 'Expectation fails where most it promises,' for it is well-nigh as impossible to exhaust as it is to describe the wonders and surprises of the Yellowstone Park."[11] Our shared image of Yellowstone National Park today grew out of the serendipitous circumstances surrounding the publication of the discovery accounts and the cascading impact of those first impressions and images.

Young grizzly bear forages for berries

EXPERIENCING YELLOWSTONE

The nature parks of the National Park Service are the system's "crown jewels." Protected from consumptive uses such as logging, hunting, and grazing, they are managed as representative bits of wild nature. They are places to experience solitude, inspiration, and beauty. They are laboratories, refugia, and museums for studying, protecting, and understanding endangered and indigenous flora and fauna. As the national park movement in this country has evolved, more and more purposes have been assigned to the parks collectively as repositories of nature and nature experiences. Equally important, however, are the meaningful experiences attached to each park individually. People go to individual parks to experience that place as much as to experience a national park.

There has been much discussion in recent decades over what sort of activities should be allowed in particular parks. There are questions regarding visitor carrying capacity, dilution of the wilderness experience, and legitimacy of tourist activities that may have low ecological impact but are somehow inappropriate (helicopter rides in Yellowstone or hang gliding in Yosemite, for example). No one argues that national parks should provide opportunities for outdoor recreation, but what types and how much are appropriate? Understanding a park's history helps answer these management questions.

In Yellowstone at the turn of the twentieth century, the only recreational activities visitors expected park administrators to provide were those associated with touring the park: traveling, "taking a cure," or merely experiencing a change of scenery and change of pace. Nowadays, Yellowstone recreational activities include everything from mountain climbing and backpacking to sailing, watching movies, and soaking in hot tubs. Certainly, the public's perception of Yellowstone as a place for recreation has evolved from a simple idea—albeit one full of possibilities—into a complex and often controversial reality. But this evolution can and should be characterized as one wherein new meanings have been

Roads and bridges as "Yellowstone Wonders." In the Northern Pacific Railroad's Wonderland 1903 pamphlet, two of the three features depicted as parts of the "Yellowstone Wonderland" are not natural. The first panel shows an erupting Old Faithful Geyser, the middle panel shows the Chittenden Bridge spanning the Yellowstone River, and the third panel shows the road and bridge through the Golden Gate Canyon southeast of Mammoth Hot Springs. Illustration reproduced courtesy of the Burlington Northern Railroad.

added to or incorporated into old ones rather than replacing old ideas with new ones.

From the moment of its discovery, Yellowstone was understood to be a place for tourists. In a speech advocating Yellowstone's designation as a national park, Langford proclaimed that "possessing adaptabilities for the highest display of artificial culture, amid the greatest wonders of nature that the world affords, beautified by the grandeur of the most extensive mountain scenery, a few years only can elapse ere the march of civil improvement will reclaim this delightful solitude, and garnish it with all the attractions of cultivated taste and refinement."[1] After the passage of the National Park Act, an editorial in *Scribner's Monthly* applauded the park's establishment, stating that Yellowstone's removal from the public domain "aims to ensure that the region shall be kept in the most favorable condition to attract travel and gratify a cultivated and intelligent curiosity."[2]

That same year, Ferdinand Hayden made his second survey of the park. Frank Bradley was a member of that expedition, and even at that early date, Professor Bradley was considering potential sites for development in the geyser basins along the Firehole River: "If a hotel were to be located in the region, the best place would probably be on the foot-hills on the east side of the river, between the Lower and Upper basins, since cold springs and abundant forage within easy reach would there be combined with dry locations for building, while the wonders and beauties of either basin would be but a short distance off."[3] Tourist development was not perceived as conflicting with the natural scene so much as complementing it. Protecting the park meant preserving "so unique an assemblage of wonders to the uses for which Nature had evidently designed them."[4]

TOURING THE PARK

Although no funds were allocated for managing Yellowstone in its enabling act, park officials and the general public soon realized that money was needed to make the park accessible. Roads, bridges, and hotels would enhance the park, making it more available to an appreciative public. One stagecoach-traveling tourist suggested that spending money to improve park roads "would cost the rich Uncle [Sam] quite a bill but it might be the means of securing what is greatly needed for the development of what nature has lavishly provided for the enjoyment of the people. It would be more sensible than much of the expensive display at banquets and funerals and public gatherings in Washington, and cost less."[5]

Travel literature soon boasted of the park's modern hotels, roadways, and bridges, all of which were considered feats of human achievement and suitable companion pieces to the region's natural architecture. Care was taken that the structures were aesthetically pleasing and suited their surroundings. Bridges accentuated the visual scene, and hotels provided comfort and elegance in the park's wild setting. Department of the Interior publications pointed out that "the chief public interest in Yellowstone centered around its spouting geysers and similar uncanny wonders of a dying volcanic region" because these were the least trouble to reach. But, "now that good roads and trails have made this great wilderness accessible, its beautiful forests, trout-filled lakes and streams, and its wild animal populations attract as many visitors as the volcanic wonders."[6] Even the hotels' locations reflected the tourist trade. Tourists traveling by horse-drawn vehicles over bumpy, steep roads and allowing time for sight-seeing, weary animals, and meals could hope to cover only twenty miles each day. This is why the park's first hotels were built twenty miles or one day's travel apart at Mammoth Hot Springs, the Fountain Paint Pots, Old Faithful, Yellowstone Lake, and the Grand Canyon.

Since the time of the discovery expeditions, visitors have expected to find a place to sleep and a nourishing meal in or around the park. In the park's early years, however, travelers often had greater expectations than could be provided, as in this description of an inn just outside the park's western boundary:

Stagecoaches wait for passengers in Gardiner, Montana. Most of Yellowstone's earliest tourists traveled to Yellowstone by rail and, at one time, had their choice of five different rail lines with which to travel. Privately owned and commercially run stagecoaches met train passengers at the railheads and provided transportation through and information about the park. Photograph courtesy of the Department of the Interior, National Park Service, Yellowstone National Park

Old Faithful Inn

The meal itself was beyond description and once eaten is never to be forgotten, for the stomach will give a lasting reminder. We were given something that looked like meat, but like the trees in Yellowstone Park, was destined never to be hewn. We would have considered it a treat had we been served with a lump of coal, a horse-blanket, a slab of marble or a keg of nails, instead of the misrepresentations that were brought to us, which only served to encourage our appetites but discourage them immediately thereafter. Drippings from the "paint pots" would have made admirable dessert instead of the mysterious petrifaction that was dished out. Sir Benkart, who has talent as a sculptor, managed by supreme effort to carve his name in the butter as a lasting monument to other wayfarers who might be destined to be caught in the web and meshes of the hostelry.[7]

As soon as the Northern Pacific and Union Pacific Railroads built spur lines to the north and west entrances of the park and invested money in tourist facilities, tourists who had the money could experience a veritable luxury in the wilderness. The Old Faithful Inn overlooking Old Faithful Geyser and the Upper Geyser Basin was built during the winter of 1903–1904 at the site of earlier hotels. East and west wings were added to the main building in 1913 and 1927, respectively, significantly increasing the number of rooms available for overnight stays. Designed by a young architect, Robert Chalmers Reamer, the Old Faithful Inn was built to reflect its setting and fit the spirit of the place—uniquely American in its log cabin–castle style; a combination of form and function, modern, comfortable, and affordable. The inn was built of native materials: rough lodgepole pine logs cut from the park's forests, massive rhyolite rock quarried in the park, and wrought iron fixtures forged at the site. Of the Old Faithful Inn, one tourist wrote:

Yet with all this rusticity, comfort, convenience and even elegance are everywhere. The polished hardwood floors are covered with oriental rugs and the furniture is of mission pattern in dark weathered oak. The windows are of heavy plate glass in leaded panes and the furnishings of the bed- and bathrooms are of the best. Yet the rustic idea is carefully maintained; even in the private rooms the walls are of rough planks or ax-dressed slabs and everything is redolent with the fragrance of the mountain pine. Verily, this inn is a pleasant place, set down as it is in a weird, enchanted land.[8]

Today, the Old Faithful Inn is as natural a component of the Yellowstone landscape as Old Faithful Geyser and grizzly bears. Despite repeated proposals to remove the hotel's additions and turn the old house (the original 1903 structure) into a museum, outcry

Mammoth Hot Springs

Horse and buggy days. National Park Service director William Penn Mott, Jr., travels in style in 1988. Photo by Judith L. Meyer

was always so great that such proposals were withdrawn. It is the public's affection for this building and its use as an inn—not a museum—that has preserved the building as part of the Yellowstone experience.

The oldest hotel still in use in the park, Yellowstone Lake Hotel, was built by the Northern Pacific Railroad from 1889 to 1891. The goal of a major renovation effort in the 1980s was to restore as much of the structure as possible to its original glory. With hardwood floors, etched glass, custom carpeting, and huge windows overlooking Yellowstone Lake, the hotel re-creates the air of elegance, sophistication, and high society unique to this location within the park. If the Old Faithful area was—and is—a place of rusticity and excitement, the lake area was—and is—a place of quiet dignity and polish.

Although many of Yellowstone's first tourists traveled on horseback or in private wagons and coaches, most arrived by rail and traveled with a group. Hence, a tradition of group travel predates the tradition of campfire talks and the creation of the National Park Service in 1916. As portrayed in the park's historical record, group travel may have been necessary since transportation facilities were rudimentary and limited, but it was also fun. The social interaction among passengers in a stagecoach became part of tourists' lasting memories of a Yellowstone experience. Stagecoach-era tourists commonly wrote about the camaraderie enjoyed during their journey through the park: "The true charm did not lie in the drive and scenery alone, but in the conversation as well. . . . The supreme pleasure came from the heart to heart talk among congenial companions."[9] Even John Muir, known for his love of solitude, remarked while traveling in Yellowstone that "among the gains of a coach trip are the acquaintances made and the fresh views into human nature; for the wilderness is a shrewd touchstone, even thus lightly approached, and brings many a curious trait to view."[10] Bouncing along over the park's rough roads,

Fireweed

stagecoach passengers had contests between groups in different coaches meeting at points of interest or while passing each other on narrow sections of road: "We had company again this evening. One crowd passed us giving the 'Montana Yell' so we fixed one up for our use on special occasions. It is 'Bear! Bear! Eat 'em up alive! Wyoming! Wyoming! Nineteen Five!'"[11] In a similar fashion today, flashing lights, honking horns, or a flutter of waving hands signals the approach of a rival tour group traveling by bus or van through the park. Motor coaches compete with one another for prime parking spaces and who can get their passengers and bags loaded and unloaded first. Group tour passengers still meet at favorite sight-seeing stops and compare and contrast sights seen, meals eaten, their drivers' skill at maneuvering the motor coach through tight squeezes, and their touring experience generally.

Some might argue that a group tour detracts from an experience of the park, since attention is focused on what is happening inside the vehicle rather than outside in the park. But such criticism assumes tourists must appreciate only the nature in the park rather than the nature of the park experience. The park's literary record is evidence of how people-oriented a Yellowstone park experience can be:

> While jogging along, our attention was attracted by vociferous singing in the rear. "Can these be cowboys on a spree?" one of the ladies anxiously asked. Soon there emerged from a dust cloud a four-horse stage, laden with a full cargo of clerical gentlemen, of no particular denomination, but smooth shaven and stout, who apparently were not paying the slightest attention to the scenery, but were making the woods fairly rattle with Sunday-school hymns.[12]

The art of traveling—not just moving from one destination to another but an appreciation for the act of traveling itself—is rooted deeply in Yellowstone's past as is the role of the driver and guide. Whether they are holding the reins on the stagecoach or the steering wheel of the touring car or motor coach, Yellowstone's drivers and guides have always figured prominently in the park experience. For example, in a Union Pacific advertisement, the railroad's promoter told of the difficulties of driving the park's mountainous roads and then asked, "How much more satisfactory to leave such things to a bus driver, who not only is thoroughly familiar with the roads in Yellowstone, but who is also an encyclopedia on the park and can point out and explain things of interest along the way!"[13] Americans, eager to believe their own "taming the wild West" mythology, endowed their drivers with qualities and characteristics they may or may not have actually possessed: "A young fellow of the refined cowboy type approached me. A very trim figure was his; the broad-brimmed, grey felt hat of the plains hung upon the back of his head like a Byzantine halo; his features were clean-cut, his complexion fresh and fair; his eyes calm, yet earnest."[14] For many tourists from overseas, stagecoach drivers personified the American West. A woman from England confided to her friends that her driver "combined the independence of America with the civility of Europe."[15] Rudyard Kipling, disdainful of the American tourist generally, may have empathized with the driver of his stagecoach when the driver admitted, "'I drive blame cur'ous kinder folk through this place,' said he. 'Blame cur'ous. Seems a pity that they should ha' come so far just to liken Norris Basin to Hell. Guess Chicago would ha' served 'em, speaking in comparison, jest as good.'"[16]

The Yellowstone travel experience has changed in many ways since the arrival of the automobile. Cars make people independent. Tourists in cars can stop and go at will, traveling at their own pace; they are not bound to prearranged schedules. One might ask, however, if the car-tourist has more of a Yellowstone experience than those opting for a group tour. Group tour participants may spend more time actually "taking in" the park than those who must search for parking spaces and service stations. Nowadays, some tourists' strongest impressions of their trip to Yellowstone include traffic jams, potholes, and the lack of parking spaces at "must see" sights.

Another aspect of traditional Yellowstone travel is the generally deplorable condition of park roads. In a passage typical of the lighthearted Carrie Strahorn—in contrast to her overzealous and ever business-oriented husband Robert—she described a noteworthy sight: "A signboard attracted our attention. It just gave the name of the plateau, but underneath some one who had evidently tried Colonel Norris' favorite road with a buggy, had added in pencil: 'Government appropriations for public improvements in the park in 1872, $35,000. Surplus on hand October 1, 1880, $34,500.'"[17] Carrie was not alone. Another author recounted the adventures of a group of the Knights Templar from Allegheny, Pennsylvania, who toured the park on their way to San Francisco late in the summer of 1904. Apparently, roads were bumpier than expected:

> Amid the clashing of the mustangs' hoofs, the yells of the driver and the report of the whip lash, any announcement that Gilland might have made was lost in the air. Fortunately, another member of the party noted our brother Sir Knight's hasty and sudden departure and induced the driver to halt long enough to gather him in. Happily, Sir Gilland was uninjured and now glories in the distinction that he is the only member of our party who saw that country during "the fall," and declares that he was more deeply touched by nature in that vicinity than any of his brother Sir Knights.[18]

Dust plagued early park travelers as well. In an interview later in her life, a woman who had toured the park in her youth explained that back then:

> the roads were full of dust around the Basin and mother had been warned that we were not to wash our faces in the park because of the dust. She made us a supply of some kind of softening water that she used. For lipstick we used the inevitable mutton tallow that was a cure

Hot water flows into the Firehole River from the Midway Geyser Basin

all for chapped lips. . . . The dust would gather on the wheels of the wagons and as we would go on it would spill out. The horses would kick up the dirt. When the wind was in the wrong direction we were just nearly smothered.[19]

For some, the dustiness and poor condition of park roads were a national disgrace:

> Everyone knows how roads in Europe climb the steepest grades in easy curves, and are usually as smooth as a marble table, free from obstacles, and carefully walled-in by parapets of stone. Why should not we possess such roads, especially in our National Park? Dust is at present a great drawback to the traveler's pleasure here; but this could be prevented if the roads were thoroughly macadamized. Surely, the honor of our Government demands that this unique museum of marvels should be the pride and glory of the nation, with highways equal to any in the world.[20]

Eventually, park roads were sprinkled with water to reduce the dust, and tourists responded approvingly: "Sprinkling from heavy, wide-tired wagons . . . keeps down the dust and packs and smooths the road, for which the tourist is profoundly grateful to Congress and to everybody connected with the improvement."[21]

At one time, features that are now regular stops on even an abbreviated park tour were virtually inaccessible due to required river crossings. But determined tourists would not be deterred by a little water. Many merely "difficult"—as opposed to "treacherous" or "impossible"—river crossings were attempted:

> Our road was a meandering one, as you will see when I tell you that we forded the last fork of Fire-Hole River five times, Willow Creek once, Trout Creek once, Alum Creek twice, and, deepest of all, a bayou of the Yellowstone once. At one crossing we gathered ourselves up on the seat and raised all the luggage, expecting the water to come up into the wagon, but we went through high and dry. I used to be afraid of such doing, but it does no good here; nobody pays the least attention to groans and sighs.[22]

It did not take park administrators long to begin building bridges, making the park easier to enjoy. The engineering feats that resulted in the modern-day road system are now taken for granted, but road building has never been easy in Yellowstone. The park's thick forests had to be cleared before roadbeds could be constructed properly. Trees were cut along the routes that would eventually become main roads, but stumps remained for years along some stretches. In the following, a traveler describes travel across land and water during his Yellowstone tour:

The first section of stumps was about eighty rods long. It was a sort of foretaste of the bliss that was to follow. . . . The coach began to rise and fall in the most unexpected manner. Up and down, crash! whang! bang! they went. I forgot that [other passengers] were in the coach. I forgot all about the other coach. I forgot about the Yellowstone Park. I nearly forgot my own name. I distinctly remembered, however, that I was in the coach. . . . The carriage-wheels were cutting the most singular antics as they flew over stumps of both low and high degree. I soon discovered that I was not resting upon the carriage-seat but a small portion of the time. The balance of it was occupied by myself in rising and falling; not graceful, perhaps, but forceful I am confident. . . . When that section was passed there was a change. This was of itself a relief, but it was change from bad to worse. We were floundering in a mud-hole so deep that the bottom had not been reached. . . . My only inspiring or consoling thought during that ride was my life insurance.[23]

Yellowstone now has a modern highway complete with exit ramps and a cloverleaf interchange. In an environment as harsh as Yellowstone's, however, the elements—rain, snow, intense heat and cold, geothermal activity, and earthquakes—keep road crews busy all year. After a century of road building and maintenance, complaints about the quality of park roads are still common. Some solace might be taken today in the knowledge that Yellowstone's travel conditions have always been less than ideal.

Perhaps an appreciation for the art of traveling at a slower and more deliberate pace fostered an awareness for a park experience more difficult to recognize today. In the past, the sequence and direction of travel were an integral part of the tour, a point to which a visitor in 1889 attested:

The route that should be followed in taking the trip is important. The tourist should not visit the points of greatest magnificence first; for then he would be in no mood to enjoy places of minor interest, seen last. Any one of the geysers, if located in Central Park, New York, would attract tens of thousands of visitors, and it would be regarded as one of the wonders of the world. Yet some of these geysers are much finer than others. They are not all in the same locality, but are scattered over a considerable area. To the majority of those who come hither, the cañon of the Yellowstone is doubtless the most wonderful location in The Park; and they should not visit it, till they have first seen and enjoyed things less interesting.[24]

The various railroads carrying tourists into the Yellowstone incorporated the idea of a proper touring sequence in their promotional literature. Apparently, viewing

Yellowstone's wonders in an orderly fashion was vital to giving meaning to the whole trip. The Union Pacific Railroad—whose spur line necessitated a long stagecoach ride to the park's western entrance—insisted that maximum enjoyment required starting at the west gate. The Northern Pacific Railroad—whose trunk line ended in Cinnabar, Montana, at the park's north gate—naturally advocated a circular route beginning and ending at the north entrance:

> First, the Mammoth Springs . . . it gives the tourist a wonderfully satisfied feeling to behold this marvelously beautiful wonder upon his very entrance to Wonderland. He is at once possessed with a satisfied feeling, confesses that he feels repaid already for the expense and trouble of the trip, and he is started on from here with a satisfied air.
>
> Next, in their order are Rustic Falls, Obsidian Cliff, Lake of the Woods, Norris Geyser Basin, Paint Pots, Monument Geyser Basin, Gibbon Cañon, Gibbon Falls, Lower Geyser Basin, and the last, the great crowning point of all wonders, the Upper Geyser Basin. By this time the tourist experiences a full sense of satisfaction, so far as the *wonderful* is concerned. He feels a strong desire to witness what in the Park may be classed more accurately under the head of the grand and beautiful; so he is taken across to the Lake. He experiences a sense of relief at getting away from the odor and sight of so much hot water. From the rest and quietness at the Lake, he is taken to the great Falls and Grand Cañon. Here the sensation is that of *quiet* wonder and amazement, while at the Geysers it is that of *excited* wonder and *delight*. At the former place he desires, as he beholds, neither to speak nor be spoken to; while at the Geysers he cannot himself refrain from shouting.[25]

Transportation traditions. Restored white touring cars are still used in the park on special occasions. The drivers' uniforms are exact replicas of the original drivers' uniforms. Photo by Judith L. Meyer

Whether to build suspense or provide relief or inspiration, the sequence of visiting each part of the park tour was essential to experiencing a grander whole. The amount of time spent in the park was crucial as well. At a time when the typical package tour took anywhere from a week to ten days due to the long train ride coupled with the slow pace of stagecoach horses once inside the park, Yellowstone promoters still warned tourists to slow down so they could "take in the essence of the park." One of John Muir's most oft-quoted passages refers to his time in Yellowstone:

> Few tourists, however, will see the Excelsior in action, or a thousand other interesting features of the park that lie beyond the wagon-roads

and the hotels. The regular trips—from three to five days—are too short. Nothing can be done well at a speed of forty miles a day. The multitude of mixed, novel impressions rapidly piled on one another make only a dreamy, bewildering, swirling blur, most of which is unrememberable.

Far more time should be taken. Walk away quietly in any direction and taste the freedom of the mountaineer. Camp out among the grass and gentians of glacier meadows, in craggy garden nooks full of Nature's darlings. Climb the mountains and get their good tidings. Nature's peace will flow into you as sunshine flows into trees. The winds will blow their own freshness into you, and the storms their energy, while cares will drop off like autumn leaves.[26]

John Stoddard said it more succinctly, although less lyrically: "the fact that it is possible to go through the Park in four or five days is not a reason why it is best to do so."[27] As roads improved and travel became more efficient, there were those who decried the faster pace of travel: "One cannot see Yellowstone in a week, although round-trip tourists hustle through it in motor busses in four days and a half. They don't see it; they glimpse it. . . . See the 'sights,' of course, and then see Yellowstone. How? Live in it. Live it. You will have the greatest experience of your life."[28]

Automobiles first arrived in Yellowstone in 1915. After two years of competition with horses and stagecoaches, automobiles replaced horses entirely. At that same time, the National Park Service was established, and the two events forever changed the way people would experience the park. The creation of a single national agency to manage a system of parks meant that Yellowstone, unique though it may be, changed from being a singular vacation destination to being one stop on a tour of several national parks. At the same time, the arrival of the automobile allowed visitors to dispense with group tours and a driver/guide. Tourists could now travel quickly and isolated from the sounds, smells, and sensations *between* park locations.

GUIDEBOOKS FOR MOTORIZED TOURISTS

Although Yellowstone "manuals for tourists" (as early guidebooks were called) changed little during the park's first half-century, their number, content, and format changed rapidly during the 1920s. Yellowstone's early tourists had few guidebooks from which to choose, but modern tourists may be overwhelmed by their choices. Many organizations—the National Parks and Conservation Association, the National Park Service, and the American Automobile Association, for example—publish national park guides as do private individuals, local merchants, and commercial publishers. Recently, video and audio cassette tapes narrated by a celebrated cast of popular faces and voices have also entered the market. This diversity and specialization

Lower Geyser Basin in winter

reflects Yellowstone's huge audience. But what of the *whole* park, its spirit of place? A wider variety of guidebooks may allow a broader appreciation of the park's many faces, but with diversification and specialization something integral—an appreciation for the whole—may have been lost.

In the 1907 and 1908 editions of the *Haynes Guide*, Congress Pool—a thermal feature in Yellowstone's Norris Geyser Basin—was described in the following manner:

> The first sight that attracts the visitor is this immense boiling spring, in close proximity to the road, on the left as you enter the basin. It is the largest spring of its class found in the Geyser Basins and is rapidly approaching a geyser. Its pale blue water is in a state of violent agitation, with occasional demonstrations that force the water fifteen or twenty feet above the rim of the crater; the diameter of the same is fully forty feet. For several years there existed near the Congress the "Steam vent," one of the features of this basin. It consisted merely of an opening in the rocks from which a great quantity of steam was constantly escaping; the roaring of the same could be heard for miles. During the winter of 1893 the "Steam vent" ceased and the Congress appeared. The first eruptions were of great force and completely blockaded the road with masses of earth and formation.[29]

Forty years later, the same feature is described in the *Haynes Guide*: "Congress Pool next to the road, usually a boiling muddy pool, sometimes a steam vent, or is quiescent."[30] The *Haynes Guide* entry for the Fountain Paint Pot changed similarly:

> In the basin is a mass of fine, whitish substance which is in a state of constant agitation. It resembles some vast boiling pot of paint or bed or mortar with numerous points of ebullition; and the constant boiling has reduced the contents to a thoroughly mixed mass of silicious clay. There is a continuous bubbling up of mud, producing sounds like a hoarsely whispered "plop-plop," which rises in hemispherical masses, cones, rings, and jets.[31]

By 1949, the mudpots' description was again reduced: "Fountain Paint Pot is a large hot caldron of clay, quartz and opal, blending in color from white to pale orange and pink."[32]

Yellowstone's earliest guidebooks were written in the form of stories or travelogues wherein the authors led readers on a journey through the park. Later, automobile-era guidebooks take on a different format so travelers can orient themselves by mile markers after stopping, starting, and changing direction. Such books are typically mile-by-mile recitations of park information. The two following entries are taken from *Haynes Guides*. Both describe Gibbon Falls, the first appeared in the 1907 edition:

Gibbon Falls, whose waters, tumbling in a foamy torrent down a series of steep cascades on one side of a bold, rocky ledge, and on the other streaming in a thin, shining ribbon of silvery spray from a height of something over eighty feet, fittingly conclude the attractions of Gibbon Canyon.

After leaving the falls the road passes for a distance of three or four miles over a succession of pine-clad terraces until it reaches the valley of the Firehole River.[33]

This second description from the 1949 edition began with numbers that indicate the distance in miles from the Norris Geyser Basin if traveling south and the distance from Madison Junction if traveling north, respectively:

> 8.80 5.20 Parking area at Gibbon Falls. These falls are 84 feet high and are beautiful both at high and low water.
> 8.95 4.30 Parking area from which Gibbon Falls may be seen. In the bank above the road is a fine example of glacial drift.[34]

Coming to experience a sense of place in Yellowstone does not require spending an entire summer in the park and depends more on the individual tourist than on his or her means of travel. However, attempts to make travel through the park ever more efficient and rapid may, ultimately and unconsciously, deter the general public from "being taken possession of by the spirit of the place." By adopting a "motorist-friendly" format, guidebooks did not change the public's image of Yellowstone so much as they reflected that change. Over time, we have allowed our sense of place to be dissected into discrete bits. Travel through the park can be calculated (to two significant digits if the mileage numbers are valid!), methodically organized, and enjoyed in separate, often unrelated, segments. The uniform format of most national park guidebooks suggests these changes are not unique to Yellowstone. Rather, people's attitudes toward travel in most of the national parks have changed. Instead of seeing each park as a single destination, a "place" to come to know, each national park is a stop on the way to another national park.

If anything about transportation and the art of traveling can be gleaned from Yellowstone's past, it is that the experience of the place has little to do with the efficiency or speed of travel. Our love of tradition is still strong. Despite the fact that more modern, comfortable, and functional vehicles are available, the original touring cars are called into service when dignitaries visit the park. Even the original uniforms have been reproduced to complement the vehicles. When William Penn Mott, Jr., then director of the National Park Service, came to Yellowstone in 1987 to dedicate a building upon the death of Horace Albright, he chose to travel—despite the rain—in one of the original horse-drawn carriages. His decision reveals respect for both the park's

This sketch entitled "Mammoth Hot Springs—Main Terrace" from W. M. Thayer's 1891 Marvels of the New West shows the trough set up to bring hot water from the active springs at the top of the mountain to the extinct cone named the Devil's Thumb in an effort to reactivate the latter.

illustrious past and our tenacious effort to preserve and relive it. Even more recently, the Park Service is hoping to reintroduce the yellow, canvas-topped touring cars of the early 1900s. These "refurbished and retrofitted" antique vehicles will run on alternative fuel so as to reduce air pollution as well as the number of cars on the roads. This nostalgic return to public transportation in the form of touring cars instead of private automobiles serves both the scientific and traditional demands of good management. Attention to both sense-of-place standards—including the importance of group travel— and attention to environmental standards—such as clean air and reduced traffic congestion—encourages innovative solutions that are ecologically correct and that satisfy our sense of tradition.

"IMPROVING" NATURE

At the time of the park's establishment, attempts to regulate elk, bison, and predator populations, to control forest fires, and to discipline park bears began almost immediately. But attempts to enhance nature did not stop there. Some of the park's first officials tried to "save" features from the natural process of erosion and decay. P. W. Norris, park superintendent from 1877 to 1882, believed Liberty Cap, an extinct hot spring at the foot of the Mammoth terraces, would soon weaken and fall. Norris first tried to strengthen the cone with wooden supports but later devised a more ingenious plan to rescue the extinct hot spring:

It therefore becomes a question of scientific as well as practical interest whether a sufficient quantity of water from the much more elevated Mammoth Hot Springs cannot be cheaply conveyed into the ancient supply-pipe of the cone, if, as seems probably, it is still open. . . . it is believed that the terrace-building properties of the water would soon encase this interesting cone with the inimitably beautiful-bordered pools of the terrace formation, and also ultimately surround it with an effective and permanent support. So strong is my conviction of the perfect feasibility of this plan, that nothing but absolute necessity of the use of all available funds for buildings and opening roads and bridle-paths has prevented my expending a moderate sum upon the experiment.[35]

Superintendent Norris was never able to replumb Liberty Cap, but he did succeed in building a trough carrying hot spring water from active springs at the top of the Mammoth terraces to a smaller inactive hot spring called the Devil's Thumb located near Liberty Cap. One tourist wrote of Norris's endeavors: "It is hoped that the deposits of time may gradually fill up the fractures and cavities, and renew the youth of the cones. It would be a pity for these mausoleums of old geysers to crumble to dust."[36] Norris's notes reveal his genuine concern and his belief in the importance of the extinct hot spring to the park experience. When Rudyard Kipling visited Yellowstone in 1889, he noticed other attempts to restore

William Henry Jackson's photograph of Liberty Cap, an extinct hot spring at the base of the Mammoth Hot Springs terraces in Hayden's Twelfth Annual Report

inactive springs and described the efforts of a cavalry officer stationed at the terraces: "He himself was devoting all his time to conserving the terraces, and surreptitiously running hot water into dried-up basins that fresh pools might form."[37]

In looking back, it is easy to label such "improvement" activities as classic examples of how many humans perceive their relationship to nature as kindly paternalistic, demeaning, or anti-wilderness and pro-technology. A century ago, however, such behavior was not necessarily based on an arrogant belief that people were superior to nature but that people and nature could coexist. "Improving" the natural landscape by making it accessible to tourists was considered a fitting and proper way to acknowledge and applaud the park's wonders.

ENGAGING IN THE ART OF PLAY

Once tourists could travel to and through Yellowstone without too much inconvenience, site-specific or park-specific recreational activities began to catch on. One such activity or behavior was the simple art of "playing." For many, the wild and curious landscape instigated childlike behavior. Even today, after one of Yellowstone's summer snowstorms, it is not unusual to find a group of tourists—senior citizens, no less—stop, disembark, and begin a snowball fight. In an earlier day, when there were fewer restrictions on what visitors could and could not do, people actively engaged in physical, playful activities usually associated with children:

> After fully enjoying the scene, we amused ourselves by rolling large rocks over the cliff. It was wonderful to see a stone the size of a trunk leap into the air in a plunge of 200 or 300 feet, strike the shelf below as if thrown by a catapult, and with such tremendous force as to rebound twenty feet, and after a series of such terrific bounds, make another tremendous leap to the slope below, continuing in bound after bound until it reached the creek. . . . While indulging in this boyish sport a faint shout came up from below signifying that there was some one down in the cañon. It is unnecessary to say that we at once stopped the stone rolling.[38]

In many ways, being in the park has always made people feel—or at least act—young, and part of that youthfulness is inquisitiveness. Reasoning adults eventually lose their need for physical, tactile proof to be convinced of a thing's existence. Once burned by a hot stove, most adults know not to touch other hot stoves. However, Yellowstone turns people into children again. Although they know hot springs are hot, people stick probing fingers into the steaming water, testing reality. Our eyes take in the clarity, depth, and color of the water and entice our fingers to feel. Despite rules forbidding such behavior and constant warnings from rangers, tourists almost instinctively pick up rocks and flowers to feel, smell, and examine them. People stop to feed birds, marmots, and ground squirrels and talk of wanting to remove socks and shoes to wade in the pools, streams, and rivers.

Yellowstone is a sensuous place, "appealing at once to sight, smell, touch, and hearing."[39] Along the Yellowstone River in the Grand Canyon, one of the park's discoverers took time to note the sensations assaulting him: "The river water here is quite warm and of a villainously alum and sulphurous taste. Its margin is lined with all kinds of chemical springs. . . . The internal heat renders the atmosphere oppressive, though a strong breeze draws through the cañon. A frying sound comes constantly to the ear, mingled with the rush of the current. The place abounds with sickening and purgatorial smells."[40] Even the sense of taste is an important part of the sensory environment. Although few tourists nowadays feel the need to sample water from the various thermal features, drinking hot spring water was at one time a typical part of coming to know the place: "I do not distinctly recall all the nasty tastes which have afflicted my palate, but I am quite sure this was one of the vilest. It was a combination of acid, sulphur and saline, like a diabolic julep of lucifer-matches, bad eggs, vinegar and magnesia. I presume its horrible taste has secured it a reputation for being good when it is down."[41]

Thermal areas, especially, stimulate the imagination and sense of fun. The sputtering of the smaller geysers and the bubbling of the mudpots elicit a variety of humorous and

Institutionalized swimming in the hot springs. By the 1920s, concessioners were allowed to set up bath houses and charge tourists to bathe in the hot spring waters that had been diverted from the formation to their facilities. This particular scene is from the Mammoth Campground in 1922, courtesy of the Department of the Interior, National Park Service, Yellowstone National Park.

often astute observations. One popular comment was that the hissing and splashing of Catfish Geyser "is not vastly different from some politicians" in that they, too, "have literally spouted themselves to exhaustion in the effort to shoot a great ball a long distance out of a small calibre."[42]

Although there are any number of landforms in the United States whose place-names incorporate the words "Devil," "Purgatory," "Hell," "Styx," "Hades," and "Satan," these terms seem appropriate in Yellowstone. The physical nature of the thermal areas conjures up images that are otherworldly or Hell-like, prompting devilish nomenclature. As if reciting a script, tourists allude to Hell or the "Nether regions," noting the sulphurous smells and bubbling sounds. These references to the devil are not so much somber and sober reminders of our own mortality as they are creative, lighthearted, and humorous, as in a description of devilish imps working the plumbing systems of the geysers and hot springs: "It requires no great flight of fancy to see in this marvelous natural mechanism a vast engine running under the guidance of a ghostly engineer, and being 'stoked' from Pluto's wood-pile by a thousand goblin firemen."[43]

Thermal features, however, were not always referred to in demonic terms. The park's hot springs, geysers, mudpots, and fumaroles were often personified. A story repeated throughout the park's history is set in a hot spring basin and pokes fun at the clergy: "One very large basin (40 × 60 feet) is filled with the most beautiful slime, varying in tint from white to pink, which blobs and spits away, trying to boil, like a heavy theologian forcing a laugh to please a friend, in spite of his natural specific gravity."[44]

Early photographs of tourists show them actively discovering and enjoying the park. Like children on a new playground, they climbed on deposits, lowered themselves into caves, fed bears, and swam in the hot pools. The suitability of Yellowstone's hot springs for swimming—especially the pools formed in the Mammoth terraces—was a long-running debate in the park's written legacy as conflicting evidence was offered on this point. In an 1882 account, Mammoth's wonderful baths were praised: "Toward evening I enjoyed a bath among the natural basins of Soda Mountain. The temperature was delightful, and could be regulated at pleasure by simply stepping from one basin to another. They were even quite luxurious, being lined with a spongy gypsum, soft and pleasant to the touch."[45] Similarly, Dr. S. Weir Mitchell sent many a troubled patient to Yellowstone to cure tired and overwrought nerves. He himself found the terrace baths both enjoyable and serviceable:

> With hundreds of gleaming bath-tubs full of water from 180°
> Fahrenheit down to 75°, the temptation to hot and tired men to bathe
> was delicious, and the only trouble lay in the difficulty of choosing our
> place. Finally, we set our hearts on a noble tub about three feet deep
> and eight in diameter. My friend, being neat in his ways, much
> rejoiced over the little dry basins about us, which he called dressing-
> tables. In one he put his brushes, in another a battered hat; in one

Mustard Spring, Biscuit Basin

soap and sponge, in another clean towels; and so on, with little clean nests for shoes and clothing worn or to be worn.[46]

During that same time, however, there were those who found the terraces neither comfortable nor practical for bathing: "We cannot leave . . . without mentioning the hot baths. All over the crusts of the different terraces are, as has been mentioned, small basins containing water of almost any temperature desired; but bathing in these pools cannot be accomplished with comfort, since the pools are almost always too shallow to admit of it."[47]

Despite the complaints, the idea of bathing at Mammoth eventually became firmly ingrained in the national consciousness as part of the Yellowstone experience. Park authorities allowed concessioners to build bathing facilities:

> A small tent is pitched a short distance from the main basin, and looking in you find an oblong hole, dug in the pure white soil, large enough to contain the human form. It is full of water, led from the spring through a trough hollowed out in the ground. This is the primitive bathing establishment of the place. They have become more luxurious out there since, and have put up several plank bath-houses, with real bath-tubs in them. The tubs are not made of white marble, nor are the floors covered with Brussels carpets;—these things will come in time. Already, these different bath-houses have established a local reputation with reference to their curative qualities. Should you require parboiling for the rheumatism, take No.1; if a less degree of heat will suit your disease, and you do not care to lose all your cuticle, take No.2. Not being possessed of any chronic disease, I chose No.3, and took one bath—no more. When I recovered I made a mental resolution never, willingly, to be a party to the cruel process of rendering lobsters edible.[48]

For a time, public bathing facilities were operated at Mammoth and near Old Faithful and fees were charged accordingly: "50 cents in large pool at Old Faithful and Mammoth; $1.00 in private pool at Old Faithful."[49] The private pool constructed at Old Faithful (the Hamilton Swimming Pool) had two pools—one for adults, one for children—and was fed with water diverted from Solitary Geyser. For many decades, swimming and wading in hot springs were a popular part of the Yellowstone experience, but the sheer number of tourists now visiting the park and a concern for public safety has led to the prohibition of such activities. Hot spring water can be dangerous, because temperatures may change quickly and without warning. Further, in keeping with attempts to restore and preserve even the tiniest of Yellowstone's ecosystems, protection was extended to the colonies of bacteria and algae living in the hot springs and their runoff channels, which are destroyed when people walk, sit, or swim in the water. Bathing in hot springs is now prohibited, but visitors can soak in several "hot pots" formed where hot water flows into cold rivers, lakes, or streams.

YELLOWSTONE'S GRIZZLY BEARS

Today, with the exception of Old Faithful Geyser, Yellowstone's bears are probably the most famous attraction associated with the park. This has not always been the case. Yellowstone National Park was not established as a game reserve, although its enabling act did call for protection against "wanton destruction" of the park's fish and game. During the first two decades of the park's existence, tourists and concessioners alike hunted in the park for food. Many early tourists came for the clearly expressed purpose of hunting elk and bear as a recreational activity. But, by the turn of the century, the nation's new concern for wildlife led to legislation protecting all park wildlife, and the thrill and necessity of the hunt were replaced by the comfort and civility of the hotel dining room.

By this time, however, bears were already immensely popular as a singular attraction. Long before gaining fame and affection as beggar bears lining park roads or waiting for handouts in parking lots and campgrounds, Yellowstone's bears were thought of as tangible evidence of Yellowstone's wildness. Jean Crawford Sharpe, who spent the summer as an eight-year-old in Yellowstone in 1909, described some of these early tourist-bear encounters:

> When the fire died down to glowing embers and "Good-night Ladies" had been sung, and it was time to turn in, the timid folk were escorted to their tents by someone carrying a kerosene lantern. (Bears were wary of lights.) . . . Bears were plentiful. Visitors from the east waited in shivering expectancy to see their first wild bear.
> This mischievous eight-year-old was often amused by planting her teddy-bear in a tree then seeking out a newly arrived "dude" and saying there was a bear in a tree just outside. Perhaps the dude was not amused at all, but maybe he felt for a moment his first thrill of danger in this wild, wild place.[50]

As bears lost their fear of humans and ventured closer to the easy food supplies available in camp and hotel garbage dumps, concessioners saw an opportunity in staging bear-feeding shows. Visitors then came to Yellowstone expecting to see bears "in the wild" feeding on restaurant and picnic garbage. Word of Yellowstone's "wild" bears spread and became an important park tradition: "For your interest and entertainment are recreation and dance halls, outdoor pageants, ranger guide and lecture service, horseback riding and nightly bear-feeding activities at the bear feeding grounds which here are frequented by a large representation of grizzlies."[51]

Not everyone evinced equal enthusiasm regarding the park bears, however. One tourist voiced a strong—although untypical—opinion: "The Yellowstone Park bears are an unmitigated and intolerable nuisance, and nine tenths of them should be killed at once."[52] Others did not oppose the bears so much as the popular notion that they were wild: "Yet the Yellowstone, for all its superb green beauty, is no howling primitive wilderness. . . . These bears are a relic of the wild, but also as authentic a product of man as the domestic horse or the garden rose. It is no easy task to preserve the old America, as the national park directors are well aware, and the bears are one of a series of carefully watched park exhibits."[53]

However, for all their profound insight, these are minority opinions. The majority of Yellowstone accounts suggest that people believed seeing bears to be a valuable, essential part of the park experience. And, although the Park Service has implemented management practices to reduce the number of human-bear encounters for three decades, people still travel to Yellowstone to see bears:

> Yellowstone's bears are vanishing from view. Not every visitor is happy with this development. I sat for a full afternoon in a ranger station and recorded some of the comments:
>
> "Do you realize I came all the way from New Jersey to see two things—Old Faithful and a real live bear in the open? I mean, look, buddy, seeing a bear running free may not mean much to you, but when you live in Weehawken, it can be a big thing in your life."[54]

Beggar bears. Grizzly and black bears once lined the roads "begging" for scraps and gave rise to the cartoon character "Yogi Bear" from Jellystone National Park. Photograph by McIntyre, courtesy of the Department of the Interior, National Park Service, Yellowstone National Park

A solitary fisherman enjoys a sunset along the Firehole River

FISH STORIES

For some, a few recreational activities have become almost synonymous with a Yellowstone vacation: geyser gazing, seeing bears, and fly-fishing. Compared with geysers and bears, the popularity of fishing may be less obvious. Home to three of the world's best trout-fishing streams, Yellowstone has always provided good fishing and is a Mecca for devout fly fishers. In the Yellowstone literature, the theme of fishing is woven throughout the historical record. Part of its fishing fame stems from an abundance of fish, notably cutthroat trout, and the supposed ease with which even beginners can hook them. Another is the quality of the setting—angling for wild trout in a free-flowing river, either close to the road or miles from the busier parts of the park. As popular as fishing is, however, it is not necessarily every Yellowstone tourist's passion, a point one tourist made very clear to his traveling companions who were avid anglers:

> I am not a fisherman. . . . I fish not, neither do I angle. It's very silly, in my estimation. I never could see the percentage of getting all dressed up in Fisherman's Disguise No.3, debating over an album of synthetic insects and sneaking up on some moron fish with a trusting disposition. . . . I'd get a better thrill casting in the ice-box for a can of sardines and landing them with a Eureka Handy Kitchen Tool, combining the features of both can-opener and egg beater.[55]

"Fishing Cone," a geyser situated in Yellowstone Lake a short distance from shore at the West Thumb Geyser Basin, has a long history as a tourist attraction. Hayden described the feature and included sketches of it in his reports: "The 'Hot Spring Cone' we called the 'Fish-Pot,' from the fact that it extended out into the lake several feet, so that one could stand on the siliceous mound and hook the trout from the cold waters of the lake, and, without moving boil them in the steaming-hot water of the spring."[56] Hayden's reference to the idea of catching and cooking a fish in one place was probably the result of a Jim Bridger story. Jim Bridger, a fur trapper who hunted and traveled through much of the greater Yellowstone area fifty years before the park was "discovered," has been credited with most of the tall tales told of the region. One such tale is that Bridger found a place in the Rockies where so many hot springs poured boiling water into a lake that the hot water formed a thick layer on top of the colder lake water. Being an astute angler, Bridger decided to hook a trout in the lake's cold, deep waters and reel it in so slowly that by the time he pulled the fish out, it was cooked![57]

By the turn of the century, catching a fish in the lake and cooking it in Fishing Cone became a park experience "without which no visit to the Park would be quite successful."[58] For the well-being of the park's human as well as aquatic inhabitants, however, this practice was deemed in later years "no longer permissible for humane reasons."[59] Nevertheless, the tradition of catching and cooking one's dinner in the same spot was a powerful and popular one—a unique Yellowstone experience—and quickly spread to other parts of the park. The hot springs along the Gardner River, in an area now referred to as "Boiling River," were also used as the setting for accounts of cooking-fish-on-the-hook activities. Hence, the Fishing Cone tradition, although it began with one particular hot spring, came to be associated with many different hot spring areas throughout the park.

Stranger still than the origin of Fishing Cone is the shorter-lived but as yet unresolved and unexplained question concerning the eerie overhead noises heard at Yellowstone Lake. In Hayden's second report on the Yellowstone region, a colleague wrote:

Fishing Cone. William Henry Holmes's sketch of "The Fish-Pot" in Hayden's Twelfth Annual Report. *This very popular sketch was included in many guidebooks, picture books, and privately published books, especially books written by individuals who had never actually toured the park or this part of Yellowstone Lake.*

> While getting breakfast, we heard every few moments a curious sound, between a whistle and a hoarse whine, whose locality and character we could not at first determine, though we were inclined to refer it to water-fowl on the other side of the lake. As the sun got higher, the sound increased in force, and it now became evident that gusts of wind were passing through the air above us, though the pines did not as yet indicate the least motion in the lower atmosphere.[60]

Hiram Chittenden included a description of this "most singular and interesting acoustic phenomenon" in the earlier editions of his book, *Yellowstone National Park*, and, in later editions, he cited scientific reports and articles published in professional journals, which described the strange occurrence. In a 1926 *Science* article, Hugh Smith recorded his observations:

> The canoe had barely gotten under way and was not more than twenty meters from the shore when there suddenly arose a musical sound of rare sweetness, rich timbre, and full volume, whose effect was increased by the noiseless surroundings. The sound appeared to come from directly overhead, and both of us at the same moment instinctively glanced upward; each afterward asserted that so great was his astonishment that he was almost prepared to see a pipe organ suspended in midair.[61]

Over the years, park visitors have likened the noises to "the ringing of telegraph wires or the humming of a swarm of bees," "a rather indefinite, reverberating sound in the sky, with a slight metallic resonance," and "atmospheric disturbance caused by violent eruptions and the liberation of gases."[62] As late as the 1940s, the *Haynes Guide* included a section on the lake's mysterious noises: "These occur when the sky is cloudless, the air perfectly still and usually in early morning. This strange noise, heard only occasionally, is not like the sound of a distant flight of birds nor any shore noise, but is weird and startling."[63] Although many tourists noted hearing the noises, many more simply alluded to them, acknowledging disappointment at having missed hearing them. Others quoted from their guidebooks the fact that the noises do exist. Hence, whether real or imagined, the overhead sounds became part of the Yellowstone experience as stories were repeated, passed on from one generation to the next.

Today, there are many activities that together constitute a Yellowstone experience. Most of these are nonconsumptive or highly regulated so as to both benefit the tourist and lessen environmental impacts. For most modern park proponents and visitors, the idea of "improving nature" with roads, hotels, or predator control goes against the current philosophy of nature preservation. In fact, the building of roads and tourist accommodations is typically cited as the reason that the national parks are being "loved to death." Historical attempts to provide recreational activities have also been blamed for the degradation of both the Yellowstone experience and the park's ecosystems. It should be recognized, however, that many of these activities were undertaken out of love for the park and its features, a desire to experience the park through touch, taste, and feel, as well as a sense of duty and honor in being able to show off the park to the American public and the world. The past should not be judged by modern standards lest we forget the rich heritage that created and continues to define Yellowstone.

THE IDEA OF THE IDEAL

The phrase "the national park ideal" is commonly used to describe the desired end product of a complex and varied history of national interests in nature preservation. There is an assumption that the evolution of the national park movement proceeded with an inherent determinism—along with science and a broadening ecological awareness—from some less-than-noble state toward a more perfect national park ideal. There is also the assumption that there actually could be an ideal national park. Such thinking and terminology create the illusion that there is, indeed, one ideal set of values to which all parks could and should conform. Little consensus exists, however, as to what an ideal park is or what its primary purposes should be. Some people travel to the parks for family sight-seeing excursions. Others use the parks for wilderness recreation. Still others see the parks as sanctuaries where human intrusion should be limited to scientific studies. Even within nature preservation organizations, dissent and disagreement are commonplace. Different people at different times have found different reasons for settling upon one or another ideal purpose or use for America's national parks.

To focus this debate rather than simply add to it, it might be helpful to revisit our understanding of evolution. Once again, Gould and Eldridge's punctuated equilibrium model offers an alternative to the stepladder approach typically associated with evolutionary change. Gould writes, "The greatest vernacular misconception of evolution views the process as an inexorable machine, working to produce optimal adaptations as best solutions to problems posed by local environments and unconstrained by the whims and past histories of organisms."[1] He suggests we abandon the notion of evolution as progressing toward a single ideal and recognize the fitness and worth of each entity, each step, within the larger process. National park management programs based on the notion that there is no single national park ideal but rather countless manifestations of our desire to preserve and protect natural landscapes offer a flexibility and consistency in management often lacking today. If each park is seen as one expression of an ideal national park, administrators could make decisions based on compatibility with sense-of-place standards rather than focusing exclusively on elusive standards of what constitutes a pristine ecosystem or a sustainable tourist economy. This alternative management philosophy encourages park officials to take park history and tourist traditions into consideration when designing management programs.

PERSONALITY AND CHARACTER OF PLACE

Yi-Fu Tuan, a geographer who has written much about the power of place, suggests that the personality of a place can have two faces: "one commands awe, the other evokes affection. . . . The personality that commands awe appears as something sublime and objective. By contrast, a place that evokes affection has personality in the same sense that an old raincoat can be said to have character."[2] The examination of accounts used in *The Spirit of Yellowstone* reveals evidence of both the park's personality and its character. Certain places and events in the park command the awe and respect of their audiences: views of the Grand Canyon and the Lower Falls, an eruption of Old Faithful, a windless day at Yellowstone Lake. At the same time, the experience of the whole park, "the totality of experience" Joseph Sax describes for all national parks, is comfortable and familiar.[3]

Too often in our attempts to describe, criticize, or manage Yellowstone as a national park, we focus on the awe-inspiring side of Yellowstone's personality. Such attention is important. It is vital that views of Yellowstone's Grand Canyon are not obstructed by buildings or obscured by air pollution and haze. It is important that grizzlies live unfenced and untamed in the Yellowstone wilderness. It is necessary for Yellowstone as a national park to be managed in such a way that its naturalness is restored and maintained in the face of the park's popularity, politics, and economics. However, we are in no immediate danger of losing the awe-inspiring experiences the park provides. Its spectacular and curious features will always attract and intrigue a devoted constituency that acts as a watchdog to protect these necessary elements of the park experience. It is the character of the park we may be in danger of losing.

WINTER

Until recently, winter has been Yellowstone's off-season. "The place is deserted by all save the hotel keepers at the hotels and the wild animals who make the Park their home."[4] One park historian suggests that winter is when the park heals or rejuvenates from the short

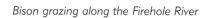
Bison grazing along the Firehole River

but intense impact of summer tourism.[5] Before the advent of personal, motorized over-the-snow vehicles, only the hardy few willing to accept the realities of Yellowstone's harsh conditions visited in winter. Most came on skis or snowshoes, made camp in the snow, traveled in silence, and found the park empty, quiet, and cold. Almost a century ago, a young army private on winter duty wrote in a letter to his sister, "Everything is so quiet that one can almost hear the solitude."[6] Echoing the sentiment, a more recent winter traveler wrote, "I was alone with my thoughts. I felt a part of something. Infinity? Creation? How can I explain it? This was something I had to feel alone."[7]

Over the past decade, Yellowstone has seen an exponential increase in winter use. Not only has the number of visitors increased, but there has been an accompanying increase in winter services available to them. Most modern winter tourists are not as self-sufficient as their predecessors. They drive snowmobiles, stay in hotels, eat in restaurants, and refuel their vehicles at gas stations. As a result, the new Yellowstone winter experience conflicts with rather than contributes to the old. This is not a situation where an aspect of the original sense of place has taken on a new dimension. Instead, the two forms of recreational park use conflict. Those who now venture into the Yellowstone winter expecting solitude and silence find crowds and the roar of snowmobiles.

Snowmobiles are fun and fast and make the park accessible when accessibility is normally limited. However, accessibility and ease of travel have never been Yellowstone's strong suits. A persistent theme reverberating through park literature is that experiencing Yellowstone is "worth the effort" of the arduous journey. Before rudimentary roads were built, even those wishing to see Yellowstone in summer had to rough it. The park's thick stands of lodgepole pine made for slow going:

> It is no easy undertaking to get here. A person must be in perfect health and strength to endure the horseback-ride over this mountain trail. I have seen some campaigning over what was called a rough country, but I must confess that I had no conception of what was involved in two hundred and fifty miles on horseback with a pack-train over the Yellowstone trail. Those weary miles, through dense thickets and over fallen timber . . . where one's eyes grow tired in looking for open spaces to crowd through; those miles of narrow trail up and down steep mountains and along the sides of cañons, where chasms yawn hundreds of feet beneath you . . . all have to be retraced on our return. But if it were ten times as long and ten times as difficult and dangerous, one sight of Old Faithful in full play, as we witnessed it to-night, and one view of this valley to the north, as I can see it now, would amply repay any one for all the difficulties to be encountered.[8]

Many tourists included descriptions of the log-strewn forests through which they alternately rode, walked, and scrambled. Others encouraged those who read their accounts

Winter light, Firehole River

to learn to tie a "diamond hitch" before heading into Yellowstone, since the diamond hitch alone would keep camping gear tied securely to a cantankerous pack mule. Olin Wheeler of the Northern Pacific Railroad regularly chastised those who believed a park tour required no preparation and effort:

> I have known of tourists, both men and women, who seemed to think that there was to be no effort required on their part to see anything: that the geysers were to be brought to them on a server; that as they sat in the coaches the falls would change position so they could be viewed without leaving their seats; that nature had provided vast deposits of asphalt, so lo! a fine asphalt pavement was spread throughout the Park. Such tourists will suffer disappointment and deserve to. While there is no hardship, there will be some fatigue. . . . As a matter of fact, when one has decided to visit the Park, practice in pedestrianism should be regularly indulged every day for a week or ten days prior to departure from home.[9]

Recently, a park ranger commented on the new type of visitor, one utterly dependent upon his or her vehicle:

> I must wonder why they need a national park for what they do, and why a national park must spend so much money to enable them to do it. . . . But still, after all the justifications and rationalizing, the [snowmobiles] still don't quite fit. It's more than a physical squeeze; they simply aren't what we have in mind for Yellowstone. It's arrogant, but we're suspicious, and I think rightly so, of all that luxury and appliance when the park is supposed to be offering simpler joys . . . the rustic element of the park experience is too far along, and too well proven, to be so lightly compromised.[10]

Certainly, there are many examples of how our sense of place for Yellowstone has modernized over time. It is hard to believe, however, that the lingering smells and sounds of snowmobiles will ever be compatible with the traditional image of Yellowstone in winter. Surely there are better places for snowmobiling than the heart of the world's oldest national park! Soon, park managers and the general public must decide which of these winter activities is essential and which is expendable to our sense of the place. Eighty years ago when the first automobiles rolled into Yellowstone, the American public was not in a position to question "appropriate use," but we are in such a position today. It may be that by removing the "effort" and making Yellowstone easily accessible in all seasons, managers will succeed in making common what is now uncommon. Yellowstone in winter will be like any other place, and that which is unique about a Yellowstone winter—its character—will simply fade away.

Corkscrew Bridge at Sylvan Pass. Photograph courtesy of the Department of the Interior, National Park Service, Yellowstone National Park

SETTING THE BOUNDARIES OF CARE AND CONCERN

The National Park Service's commitment to protecting Yellowstone should include preserving those parts of Yellowstone's historical landscape that lie outside the park's physical, legal boundaries. Typically, a trip to Yellowstone does not begin when one crosses into the park. Instead, it begins miles or hundreds of miles from the park and often years in advance of the actual visit. Obviously, such measures of time and space are outside the purview of park managers. However, the NPS should be able to regulate, at least to some degree, the status of lands bordering the park. If the park's historical record is included in management decisions, prominent landmarks, landforms, and even roadways could be considered part and parcel of the Yellowstone experience.

Paradise Valley and Emigrant Peak

Most guidebook authors—especially those associated with the Northern Pacific Railway whose spur line bisected the area—and many tourists mention Paradise Valley, the lovely, gently rolling, open valley of the lower Yellowstone River between the park's north entrance and Livingston, Montana. When Yellowstone's boundaries were drawn, the valley was never considered part of the preserve, since its fertile, easily irrigated soils had already attracted settlers.

Local small-scale farms, gold mines, and tourist facilities have long been a part of Paradise Valley. And the mountains enclosing the valley have long caused many Yellowstone-bound travelers to pause. Emigrant Peak, the highest peak in the Snowy Mountains, stands out on the landscape and in the park's written record as early as the discovery accounts. In his lecture tours, Langford re-created for his audience the experience of watching a mountain storm on Emigrant Peak:

> An exhibition of mountain phenomena, common in Montana greeted our eyes as we passed the Pyramid. A black cloud enveloped its summit casting its gloomy shadow over the adjacent peaks, and burst into a grand storm of more than an hour's duration when the vapors slowly receded, and the mountain emerged from them, bathed in a glow of sunlight. The magnificent changes in mountain scenery, occasioned by light and shade, during one of these terrific tempests, with all the incidental accompaniments of thunder, lightning, rain, snow and hail, must be seen to be appreciated.[11]

Ferdinand Hayden, awed by the peak's beauty and geology, wrote about both as well as the value of the whole mountain range as a source of water for the surrounding region: "This range . . . forms the great watershed between two portions of the Yellowstone River . . . and gives origin to some of the most important branches of that river. Large numbers of springs and small streams flow down from the mountains into the Yellowstone on the southwest side . . . the Big Bowlder, Rosebud, Clark's Fork, and Pryor's Fork, with their numerous branches."[12] However, as the modern world rediscovers the Yellowstone area, retirement and second home subdivisions and large-scale tourism are claiming more and more public and private lands. It is absurd to suggest that the whole valley be annexed to Yellowstone, but the austerity of Emigrant Peak and the middle landscape of Paradise Valley are historically significant as a route of passage into the Yellowstone. It may be wise for local and federal planners to plan now for the sort of future they envision for this gateway corridor to Yellowstone National Park.

Cody Road

"The Cody Road," or, as the Lions Club of Cody, Wyoming, would have us believe, the "most scenic seventy miles in the world" connects Cody with Yellowstone's east entrance.[13] A very different landscape greets those who enter Yellowstone from the east. Rather than the green fields of Paradise Valley, the Cody Road is dry and rugged. It is a landscape of fantastically shaped rocks, the North Fork of the Shoshone River, and the Shoshone National Forest, the country's oldest national forest. If guidebooks are any indication, the Shoshone lands—forest, rocks and river—are yet more of Yellowstone's treasures. The *Haynes Guide* and its contemporaries encouraged sightseers to find various shapes expertly carved by wind and water in the walls of the North Fork canyon. Among them were the Holy City, the Wooden Shoe, Ptarmigan Mountain, Thor's Anvil, and the Mutilated Hand. Members of the Cody Lions Club added other caricatures to the list: the Laughing Pig, the Bear, and the Goose, as well as the Old Fashioned Lady, the Devil's Elbow, the Playground of the Gods, and the Garden of the Goops. The Northern Pacific Railroad warned its passengers that "to visit Yellowstone without seeing the Cody Road is comparable to going all the way to New York and then coming away without seeing Broadway or Fifth Avenue. It is the 'show road' to or from the Park."[14]

Just inside the park's east entrance, the road rises quickly into the Absaroka Mountains and up and over Sylvan Pass. These steep grades were a formidable obstacle to tourists traveling in horse-drawn vehicles, but civil engineers came to their rescue by constructing "corkscrew bridges." To decrease the grade by increasing distance, these spiraling bridges helped ease the strain on horses and mules by gently lifting them up to the pass. One stagecoach driver known for his "truthful lies" described a corkscrew bridge as so crooked and twisted that "you pass one place three times before you get by it, and then meet yourself on the road coming back."[15] All of Yellowstone's corkscrew bridges are now gone. Some were removed and replaced with modern bridges. Others were left by the side of the road when modern, macadamized roads were laid nearby on slopes graded for automobile traffic. Like stagecoaches and silent winters, corkscrew bridges are quickly passing from the public's memory of a Yellowstone experience.

Once the corkscrew bridges were built, however, the Cody Road became a popular route to the park, especially for Wyoming residents who stopped in Cody for supplies. For them, it was at this point, in Cody, that their Yellowstone adventure began:

> Wednesday morning we started on for the Park which, we were told, was still sixty four miles distant. We were now approaching the mountains and had passed through some gorgeous scenery. The road was lined with travelers in wagons, in carriages, in coaches and on horseback, going to and from the Park . . . Our road led us up the North Fork, the scenery of which thrilled us to the toes after our three weeks' sight seeing of sage brush and sandy wastes.[16]

In recent years, residents of the Shoshone region along with concerned individuals from across the United States have worked together to designate the North Fork of the Shoshone River as wild and scenic. Such status secures the river's naturalness by severely restricting future development or use of the stream and its environs. This designation also reconfirms the North Fork's image as a natural feature worth preserving for public rather than private interests. Hence, in the public's mind, as well as in the eyes of the law, the corridor along the Cody Road through the Shoshone National Forest and into Yellowstone National Park is a part of the larger region of concern known as Yellowstone.

The Devil's Slide

The Devil's Slide is a Yellowstone classic, figuring prominently in the park's historic record. In his discovery account, Langford introduced Devil's Slide to his readers: "In future years, when the wonders of the Yellowstone are incorporated into the family of fashionable resorts, there will be few of its attractions surpassing in interest this marvelous freak of the elements."[17] And, as predicted, future tourists did see the odd, geologic feature as their first taste of many wonders lying in the strange and intriguing land just ahead. However, despite the fact that most people assume the Slide belongs to Yellowstone National Park, it lies just outside the park boundary on private land belonging to the Church Universal and Triumphant (CUT), a religious sect headquartered near the park's northern border. The Slide is not accessible to the general public, although it can be seen from across the Yellowstone River. Currently, the Slide is fenced off with barbed wire to contain cattle that graze on surrounding CUT lands. In 1980, millionaire Malcolm Forbes owned the Devil's Slide and what is now the CUT ranch, and he offered to sell the land to the federal government at that time. However, after negotiations fell through, the land was sold to CUT, and the Devil's Slide slipped out of the hands of Yellowstone managers.

Midway Geyser Basin

Grasshopper Glacier

Grasshopper Glacier is another natural feature that is "part and parcel of the wonders of the Park region."[18] Grasshopper Glacier, so named because grasshoppers are visible, frozen in the glacier's ice, is not located in or near the park but in the Beartooth Wilderness Area in the Absaroka Mountains to the northeast. Despite its distance from the park, the *Haynes Guide* included this description: "The Grasshopper Glacier! This extraordinary natural phenomenon just across the park line, fits well in the scheme of the great wonderland."[19]

In no immediate danger of development or private ownership, Grasshopper Glacier is included here as an example of how ill-defined and subjective the perceptual boundaries delineating the Yellowstone are. It is no wonder, then, that the various groups voicing concern over their interests in the "Greater Yellowstone" have as many different mental maps and agendas as to what comprises the Greater Yellowstone as they have proposals for its management. The park's history can provide valuable and viable evidence supporting or disproving claims as to what has been traditionally considered a part of the park experience.

PRESERVING CHARACTER

In 1904, the McLaughlin family traveled to Yellowstone by horse and buggy. Forty years later, after visiting the park again, Carrie Todd McLaughlin—wife and mother of the clan—recorded their experiences "in order to preserve these notes in permanent form and in sufficient number to permit each one interested to have a copy":

> We . . . went over the same route, this time by automobile, covering in three days the mileage that before had required five weeks. In the Park we found but little change; cabins had replaced the camping facilities, and the number of tourists had multiplied many fold; some of the geysers had ceased to flow, while others had broken out. But the Black Growler still growls as fiercely; Old Faithful still throws up every sixty three minutes; the colors of the cañon are as vivid; the cataracts are as awe-inspiring and the odor of sulphur pervading the atmosphere is still as overpowering.[20]

In the one hundred and twenty-five years since its establishment, Yellowstone has matured, but in many ways it has not really changed. A strong sense of place experienced by millions of park visitors has persisted over the course of the park's dramatic history. However, the management emphasis now placed on science, economics, and politics may desensitize us and keep us from experiencing both the personality and character of the park. If park managers do not recognize and defend Yellowstone's character, the Yellowstone experience may become a generic vacation in a contrived wilderness setting. Scientific management based on some ambiguous state of ecological health cannot predict public opinion, nor can science explain people's attraction to and affection for the place. Science and ecological standards are and should always be important tools in the management of any natural area, but science alone cannot and should not inject values into the decision-making process. An understanding of a park's history is important, too. "National parks do have scientific purposes," writes Tom Vale, geographer and historian of the national parks. Parks "represent the best opportunity to protect nature in the world." But they do more. National parks "have humanistic purposes as well, such as exploring our pasts, expanding our knowledge, stretching our muscles, inspiring our emotions, renewing our psyches, and encouraging economics."[21]

A humanistic perspective on park management has implications for other national parks, especially the handful of truly wild places in the national park system. The sense of place we associate with Alaskan parks, for example, conjures up images of inaccessible, pristine, austere environments. If Yellowstone represents an ideal national park and accommodates more than three million visitors each summer, what does this suggest for the future of Denali, Gates of the Arctic, and Wrangell–St. Elias National Parks? Recognizing national parks as entities rather than potential ideals may save some parks from becoming humanized.

A humanistic perspective allows an appreciation for the constraints and opportunities unique to each park, and achieving "the national park ideal" becomes a task of balancing change and permanence, science and history, in parks individually rather than collectively. We must move away from seeing Yellowstone as "the ideal" national park and as a model for management practices in all parks. Other parks have equally important, albeit different, histories and personalities and are "places" in their own right. Their designation as national parks represents other, equally valid points on the continuum of our evolving appreciation for nature. These parks should be managed so as to emphasize their personalities—their spirits of place—rather than emulating Yellowstone.

There is still much to be learned about Yellowstone. And, models describing biological evolution cannot explain culture and cultural artifacts such as national parks. The punctuated equilibrium model, however, does point out the importance of non-change and the importance of initial conditions: aspects of evolution we have tended to ignore. Biological evolution differs from cultural evolution, however, because people can actively and purposefully alter the course of cultural change. Not only can we give meanings to the world around us and thereby create places, we also have the power to control cultural forces—economic constraints, political agendas, and scientific and technological capabilities. We can make decisions that will determine our future.

In the national parks, we need to be aware of the limits we set when we insist that the main goal of park management is to protect bits of nature. Attitudes toward nature change over time. Should our attitudes toward national parks change as well? *The Spirit of*

Yellowstone is an attempt to bring part of Yellowstone National Park's past—and thereby its present—to light by reconsidering the importance of the park's written record and the traditions it fostered. The perspective introduced here focuses on Yellowstone's history as place, as a shared geographic and cultural reality, and the powerful and persistent sense of place we experience there. There are strong ties that have long bound us to this place, and Yellowstone's patterns of continuity are at least as strong as its patterns of change. Let us hope that Yellowstone's future is as meaningful and inspiring as its past.

Bull elk and harem near the Gibbon River

NOTES

INTRODUCTION

1. Dorr G. Yeager, *Your Western National Parks* (New York: Dodd, Mead and Co., 1947), 53.

REVOLUTIONARY IDEAS AND EVOLUTIONARY PROCESSES

1. At the time of Yellowstone's establishment, much of what is now Yosemite National Park had already been set aside by the federal government as a state park, and there are those who rightfully argue that Yosemite is the first national park in the United States. However, the Yosemite Park Act of 1864 called for Yosemite to be administered by the state of California, whereas Yellowstone was established as a national or federal preserve, not a state preserve.
2. Lewis R. Freeman, *Down the Yellowstone* (London: William Heinemann, 1923), 29–30.
3. Wallace Stegner, "The Marks of Human Passage," in *Mirror of America*, ed. David Harmon (Boulder, Colo.: Roberts Rinehart, 1989), 169.
4. See Stephen Jay Gould, "Opus 2000," *Natural History* 100, no. 8 (August 1991): 12–18.
5. Ronald A. Foresta in *America's National Parks and Their Keepers* (Washington, D.C.: Resources for the Future, 1984), for example, recognizes three political or administrative eras: the Mather–Albright era (1891–1920s), the Roosevelt–Kennedy era (1930s–1960s), and the modern era (1960s–present). Alfred Runte in *National Parks: The American Experience* (Lincoln: University of Nebraska Press, 1979) is less exacting in designating time spans but divides the history of the national parks into eras defined by public motivation for creating parks.
6. Robert Barbee and Paul Schullery, "Yellowstone: After the Smoke Clears," *National Parks* 63, nos. 3–4 (March/April 1989): 18.
7. For the most comprehensive bibliography of historical documents pertaining to Yellowstone National Park, see Lee H. Whittlesey, *Wonderland Nomenclature: A History of the Place Names of Yellowstone National Park* (Helena: Montana Historical Society Press, 1988).

8. A complete list of sources is included in the bibliography.
9. A. C. Peale in Ferdinand V. Hayden, *Sixth Annual Report of the United States Geological Survey of the Territories* (Washington, D.C.: GPO, 1873), 160.
10. Marshall in Robert A. Strahorn, *To the Rockies and Beyond* (Chicago: Belford, Clarke and Co., 1881), 212.
11. A. M. Mattoon, "The Yellowstone National Park, Summer of 1889," handwritten journal (Yellowstone Park Research Library, Mammoth Hot Springs, Wyo., 1917), 99.
12. Cornelius Hedges, "Journal of Judge Cornelius Hedges," *Contributions to the Historical Society of Montana* 5 (1904): 378.
13. Edwin J. Stanley, *Rambles in Wonderland* (New York: D. Appleton and Co., 1880), 60.
14. Earl of Dunraven, *The Great Divide* (London: Chatto and Windus, 1876), 331.
15. William M. Thayer, *Marvels of the New West* (Norwich, Conn.: Henry Bill Publishing, 1888), 82.
16. Rose Lambert Price, *A Summer in the Rockies* (London: Sampson Low, 1898), 180.
17. Alma White, *With God in the Yellowstone* (Zaraphath, N.J.: Pillar of Fire, 1933), 53.
18. Cal C. Clawson, "The Region of the Wonderful Lake—Yellowstone," *New Northwest* (Deer Lodge, Mont.), 18 May 1872, 20.
19. Thompson P. McElrath, *The Yellowstone Valley* (St. Paul, Minn.: Pioneer Press, 1880), 99.
20. Clawson, "Region," 2.
21. Olin D. Wheeler, *Wonderland '97* (St. Paul, Minn.: Northern Pacific Railway, 1897), 43.
22. W. C. Riley, *Official Guide to the Yellowstone National Park* (St. Paul, Minn.: W. C. Riley, 1889), 72–73.
23. George W. Wingate, *Through the Yellowstone Park on Horseback* (New York: O. Judd, 1886), 88–89.
24. Almon Gunnison, *Rambles Overland* (Boston: Universalist Publishing House, 1884), 49.
25. Marie M. Augspurger, *Yellowstone National Park* (Middletown, Ohio: The Naegele-Auer, 1948), 1.
26. James C. Fennell, "In the Yellowstone Park," *California Illustrated* 2, no. 3 (1892): 362–63.
27. Otto Zardetti, *Westlich! oder Durch den fernen Westen Nord-Amerikas* (Mainz, Denmark: Verlag von Franz Kirchheim, 1887), 49.
28. Ferdinand V. Hayden, "The Wonders of the West—II," *Scribner's Monthly* 3, no. 4 (1872): 389.
29. Ferdinand V. Hayden, *Preliminary Report of the U.S. Geological Survey of Montana and Portions of Adjacent Territories; Being a Fifth Annual Report of Progress* (Washington, D.C.: GPO, 1872), 76.
30. Union Pacific System, *Geyserland* (Omaha, Nebr.: W. H. Murray, 1923), 13.
31. Theodore Gerrish, *Life in the World's Wonderland* (Biddleford, Maine: Privately published, 1886), 194.
32. Northern Pacific Railway, *The Way to Wonderland: Yellowstone National Park* (St. Paul, Minn.: Northern Pacific Railway, 1935), 25.
33. J. E. Williams, "Vacation Notes: Summer of 1888: Through the Yellowstone Park," *Amherst (Mass.) Record,* 1888, 12.
34. James Richardson, *Wonders of the Yellowstone Region* (London: Blackie, 1876), 2.
35. John H. Raftery, "Historical Sketch of Yellowstone National Park," *Annals of Wyoming* 15, no. 2 (1943): 125.
36. L. Gannett, *Sweet Land* (Garden City, N.Y.: Doubleday, Doran and Co., 1934), 171.
37. Paul Schullery, *Mountain Time* (New York: Simon and Schuster, 1988), 39.
38. Dunraven, *Great Divide*, 188.
39. Hiram M. Chittenden, *The Yellowstone National Park* (Cincinnati, Ohio: R. Clarke, 1895), 189.
40. Ray S. Baker, "A Place of Marvels: Yellowstone Park as It Now Is," *Century Magazine* 66, no. 4 (August 1903): 490.

41. Wallace Smith, *On the Trail in Yellowstone* (New York: G. P. Putnam, 1924), 16–17.
42. John L. Stoddard, *John L. Stoddard's Lectures*, vol. 10 (Boston: Balch Brothers, 1898), 208.
43. Reverend Talmage in Charles H. Gates, *Yellowstone National Park, Alaska and the White Pass* (Toledo, Ohio: Franklin Printing, 1903), 9.
44. Editors of *Scribner's Monthly*, "The Yellowstone National Park," *Scribner's Monthly* 4, no. 1 (May 1872): 121.
45. John L. Stoddard, *Lectures*, 255–56.
46. Joe Chapple, *A' Top o' the World* (Boston: Chapple Publishing, 1922), 10.
47. Wingate, *Through Yellowstone Park*, 74–75.
48. Schullery, *Mountain Time*, 163.
49. Jim Carrier, *Letters from Yellowstone* (Boulder, Colo.: Roberts Rinehart, 1987), 54–55.
50. Montana Department of Agriculture and Publicity, *Resources and Opportunities of Montana* (Helena, Mont.: Independent Publishing Company, 1918), 104.
51. John Muir, *Our National Parks* (Madison: University of Wisconsin Press, 1981), 59.
52. Schullery, *Mountain Time*, 162.
53. Gustavus C. Doane in *Battle Drums and Geysers*, ed. Orrin H. Bonney and Lorraine Bonney (Chicago: Swallow Press, 1970), 332.
54. Hayden, *Preliminary Report*, 162.
55. Schullery, *Mountain Time*, 169.

THE DISCOVERY ACCOUNTS

1. For discussions of who was the first to enter the Yellowstone region, see Merrill J. Mattes, "Behind the Legend of Colter's Hell: The Early Exploration of Yellowstone National Park," *Mississippi Valley Historical Review* 36 (1949): 251–82; Aubrey L. Haines, *The Yellowstone Story*, 2 vols. (Boulder: Colorado Associated Press, 1975); Joel C. Janetski, *Indians of the Yellowstone Park* (Salt Lake City, Utah: Bonneville Books, 1987); and Fred R. Gowans, *A Fur Trade History of Yellowstone Park* (Orem, Utah: Mountain Grizzly Publications, 1989).
2. For information on the origin of place-names within the park, see Lee H. Whittlesey, *Yellowstone Place Names* (Helena: Montana Historical Society Press, 1988). For information on the park's current and past road systems, see Bob R. O'Brien, "The Future Road System of Yellowstone National Park," *Annals of the Association of American Geographers* 56, no. 3 (1966): 385–407.
3. Joseph Weixellman, "The Power to Evoke Wonder: Native Americans and the Geysers of Yellowstone National Park" (Master's thesis, Montana State University, 1992).
4. See especially W. Turrentine Jackson, "The Creation of Yellowstone National Park," *Mississippi Valley Historical Review* 29 (1943): 187–88; Hans Huth, *Nature and the American* (Berkeley: University of California Press, 1957); Orrin H. and Lorraine Bonney in *Battle Drums and Geysers* (Chicago: Swallow Press, 1970); Roderick Nash, *Wilderness and the American Mind* (New Haven, Conn.: Yale University Press, 1975); Haines, *Yellowstone Story*; John Ise, *Our National Park Policy* (Baltimore: Johns Hopkins University Press, 1985); Alfred Runte, *National Parks* and *Yosemite: The Embattled Wilderness* (Lincoln: University of Nebraska Press, 1990); Horace M. Albright, *The Birth of the National Park Service* (Salt Lake City: Howe Brothers, 1985); and Richard A. Bartlett, *Yellowstone: A Wilderness Besieged* (Tucson: University of Arizona Press, 1985).
5. Yi-Fu Tuan, "Language and the Making of Place: A Narrative-Descriptive Approach," *Annals of the Association of American Geographers* 81, no. 4: 684–96.
6. See N. P. Langford in David E. Folsom, "The Folsom-Cook Exploration of the Upper Yellowstone in the Year 1869," *Contributions to the Historical Society of Montana* 5 (1904): 348–69; Jackson, "Creation"; Aubrey Haines in Charles W. Cook, David E. Folsom, and William Peterson, *The Valley of the Upper Yellowstone* (Norman: University of Oklahoma Press,

1965); Bonney, *Battle Drums*; Joe B. Frantz, "The Meaning of Yellowstone," *Montana Magazine of Western History* 22, no. 3 (July 1972): 5–11; Haines, *Yellowstone Story*; Bartlett, *Wilderness Besieged*.

7. Haines, *Yellowstone Story*, 84.

8. Haines, *Yellowstone Story*, 101.

9. N. P. Langford, "The Wonders of the Yellowstone, Part Two," *Scribner's Monthly* 2, no. 2 (June 1871): 113–29; see also Walter Trumbull, "The Washburn Yellowstone Expedition, Number Two," *Overland Monthly* 6, no. 6 (June 1871): 489–96.

10. Hayden, *Preliminary Report*, 79, 82 and 94–95, respectively.

11. Frances Fuller Victor, *The River of the West* (Oakland, Calif.: Brooks-Sterling, 1974), 75. Whether Meek or another early Yellowstone visitor came up with the "Pittsburgh" analogy is debatable. Victor admits to using outside sources in reconstructing parts of Meek's life. It is likely that various articles in *The Montana Post*, a newspaper published in Virginia City, Montana, provided a good portion of Meek's supposed commentary on the Yellowstone region.

12. Hayden, *Preliminary Report*, 112.

13. Ferdinand von Hochstetter, *Neu=Seeland* (Stuttgart, Germany: Cotta'scher Verlag, 1863), 260.

14. Ferdinand von Hochstetter [translated] in Hayden, *Preliminary Report*, 176.

15. Hayden, *Preliminary Report*, 67 and 65; Hayden, "Wonders," 390.

16. Peale in Hayden, *Preliminary Report*, 174.

17. Peale in Ferdinand V. Hayden, *Sixth Annual Report of the United States Geological Survey of the Territories* (Washington, D.C.: GPO, 1873), 125.

18. N. P. Langford, "The Ascent of Mount Hayden," *Scribner's Monthly* 6, no. 2 (June 1873): 157.

19. Langford, "Wonders, Part Two," 128.

20. Hayden in Bonney, *Battle Drums*, 422.

21. Gustavus C. Doane, "The Report of Lieutenant Gustavus C. Doane upon the So-called Yellowstone Expedition of 1870," 41st Cong., 3rd sess., 1871, Sen. Exec. Doc. No. 51, 16.

22. Hayden, *Preliminary Report*, 92.

23. Langford, "Wonders, Part Two," 125.

24. Doane, "The Report of Lt. Doane," 31.

25. Henry D. Washburn in Bonney, *Battle Drums*, 216.

26. Folsom, "Folsom-Cooke Exploration," 363.

27. Gunnison, *Rambles Overland*, 30–31.

28. N. P. Langford, "The Wonders of the Yellowstone, Part One," *Scribner's Monthly* 2, no. 1 (May 1871): 9.

29. Clawson, "The Region," 14.

30. A. M. Cleland, *Through Wonderland* (Chicago: Rand McNally, 1910), 19.

31. Robert E. Strahorn, *To the Rockies and Beyond* (Chicago: Belford, Clarke and Co., 1881), 79.

32. Edmund Frederick Erk, *A Merry Crusade to the Golden Gate* (Akron, Ohio: Werner, 1906), 42; Carrie Adell Strahorn, *Fifteen Thousand Miles by Stage* (New York: G. P. Putnam, 1911), 419.

33. J. H. Beadle, *The Undeveloped West* (Philadelphia: National Publishing, 1873), 678.

34. Robert E. Strahorn, *The Enchanted Land* (Omaha, Nebr.: New West Publishing, 1881), 31.

35. Williams, "Vacation Notes," 8.

36. W. W. Wylie, *Yellowstone National Park* (Kansas City, Mo.: Ramsey, Millett, and Hudson, 1882), 1.

37. Flora Chase Pierce, Letter dated 8 August 1897 (Yellowstone Research Library, Mammoth Hot Springs, Wyo., 1897), n.p.

38. Margaret Andrews Cruikshank, "A Lady's Trip to Yellowstone in 1883: 'Earth Could Not Furnish Another Such Sight,'" in *Montana Magazine of Western History* 39, no. 1 (winter 1989): 11.

39. Cruikshank, "Lady's Trip," 4.

40. Wingate, *Through the Yellowstone*, 94.

41. Henry J. Winser, *The Great Northwest* (New York: G. P. Putnam, 1883), 31.

42. Edwards Roberts, *Shoshone and Other Western Wonders* (New York: Harper and Brothers, 1889), 234.

43. Stanley, *Rambles*, 98.

44. Edward Marston, *Frank's Ranche or My Holiday in the Rockies* (London: Sampson Low, 1886), 121–22.

45. Doane, "The Report," 282.

46. William E. Strong, *A Trip to the Yellowstone National Park in July, August, and September, 1875*, ed. Richard A. Bartlett (Norman: University of Oklahoma Press, 1968), 49. Gustavus Doane accompanied General W. E. Strong's Yellowstone expedition of 1875, so it is possible that Strong learned of the "sun being blocked out" directly from Doane rather than from Doane's published journal.

47. Gerrish, *World's Wonderland*, 224.

48. Dunnell in Hayden, *Preliminary Report*, xviii–xix.

49. Wingate, *Through the Yellowstone*, 11; italics mine.

50. Chittenden, *Yellowstone Park*, 209–10.

51. Olin D. Wheeler, *Wonderland 1906* (St. Paul, Minn.: Northern Pacific Railway, 1906), 24.

FOLLOWING IN THE FOOTSTEPS

1. For example, the frozen cascade phrase appears in Richardson, *Yellowstone Region*; William C. Bryant, *Picturesque America*, 2 vols. (New York: D. Appleton and Co., 1872); Henry J. Norton, *Wonderland Illustrated* (Virginia City, Mont.: Harry J. Norton, 1873); Dunraven, *Great Divide*; Stanley, *Rambles*; Strahorn, *Enchanted Land*; L. P. Brockett, *Our Western Empire* (Philadelphia: Bradley, 1881); and Winser, *Great Northwest*.

2. Archibald Geikie, *Geological Sketches at Home and Abroad* (New York: Macmillan, 1892), 222.

3. Philetus W. Norris, *Calumet of the Coteau* (Philadelphia: J. B. Lippincott, 1884), 70.

4. Edward Pierrepont, *Fifth Avenue to Alaska* (New York: G. P. Putnam, 1884), 243.

5. H. Credner, "Der National-Park am Yellowstone," *Geographischer Zeitschrift* 1 (1895): 85.

6. Hayden, *Preliminary Report*, 70.

7. Hayden, *Preliminary Report*, 69.

8. Dunraven, *Great Divide*, 196.

9. Langford, "Wonders, Part One," 9.

10. Hayden, *Preliminary Report*, 78–79.

11. J. W. Clampitt, *Echoes from the Rocky Mountains* (Chicago: Belford, Clarke and Co., 1889), 559.

12. Doane, "The Report," 8.

13. Doane in Bonney, *Battle Drums*, 340.

14. Gunnison, *Rambles Overland*, 39.

15. Doane, "The Report," 29.

16. Hayden, *Preliminary Report*, 121.

17. Norton, *Illustrated*, 13; Rossiter Raymond in Brockett, *Western Empire*, 1259. Other guidebook authors who copied part or all of Doane's report in the geyser basins were Winser, *Great Northwest*; Riley, *Official Guide*; and Chittenden, *Yellowstone Park*.

18. See Thurman Wilkins, *Thomas Moran: Artist of the Mountains* (Norman: University of Oklahoma Press, 1966) and Amy O. Bassford and Fritiof Fryxell, eds., *Home-Thoughts, from Afar* (East Hampton, N.Y.: East Hampton Free Library, 1967).

19. Hayden 1872, *Preliminary Report*, 124 and 122, respectively.

20. Doane, "The Report," 31–32.

21. J. W. Barlow and D. P. Heap, "Report of a Reconnaissance of the Basin of the Upper Yellowstone in 1871," 42nd Cong., 2nd sess., 1872, Sen. Exec. Doc. 66, 31.
22. John Gibbon, "The Wonders of the Yellowstone," *Journal of the American Geographical Society of New York* 5, no. 99 (1878): 135–36.
23. Olin D. Wheeler, *Wonderland '96* (St. Paul, Minn.: Northern Pacific Railroad, 1896), 68.
24. Olin D Wheeler, *Wonderland '98* (St. Paul, Minn.: Northern Pacific Railroad, 1896), 70.
25. Riley, *Official Guide*, 60–61.
26. J. A. I. Washburn, *To the Pacific and Back* (New York: Sunshine, 1887), 166.
27. Strahorn, *Enchanted Land*, 14–15.
28. Gerrish, *World's Wonderland*, 208.
29. Strahorn, *Fifteen Thousand Miles*, 260.
30. Langford, "Wonders, Part One," 12.
31. Riley, *Official Guide*, 57.
32. Hoyt in Brockett, *Western Empire*, 1241.
33. Hayden, *Preliminary Report*, 83–84.
34. Hoyt in Brockett, *Western Empire*, 1242.
35. Talmage in Elia W. Peattie, *A Journey through Wonderland* (St. Paul, Minn.: Northern Pacific Railroad, 1890) 33 and 31, respectively.
36. Peattie, *Journey*, 34.
37. Stanley, *Rambles*, 77.
38. Rudyard Kipling, *American Notes: Rudyard Kipling's West*, ed. Arrell Morgan Gibson (Norman: University of Oklahoma Press, 1979), 112.
39. Caroline L. Paull, "Notes on Yellowstone National Park, June 28–August 4, 1897," Manuscript (Yellowstone Park Research Library, Mammoth Hot Springs, Wyo., 1897), 4.
40. Wingate, *Through the Yellowstone*, 131.
41. Langford, "Wonders, Part One," 13.
42. Langford, "Wonders, Part One," 13.
43. Doane, "Report of Lt. Doane," 13.
44. J. W. Barlow and D. P. Heap, "Report of a Reconnaissance of the Basin of the Upper Yellowstone in 1871," 42nd Cong., 2nd sess., 1872, Sen. Exec. Doc. No. 66, 14.
45. Dunraven, *Great Divide*, 222.
46. Winser, *Great Northwest*, 70.
47. Olin D. Wheeler, *6,000 Miles Through Wonderland* (St. Paul, Minn.: Northern Pacific Railroad, 1893), 82.
48. Folsom, "Folsom-Cooke Exploration," 367.
49. Charles Warner, "Editor's Study," in *Old Yellowstone Days*, ed. Paul Schullery (Boulder: Colorado Associated University Press, 1979), 163.
50. Wheeler, *Wonderland '97*, 53–54.
51. Hayden, *Preliminary Report*, 96.
52. Rossiter W. Raymond, *Camp and Cabin* (New York: Fords, Howard, and Hulbert, 1879), 204.
53. Stephen Jay Gould, "The Creation Myths of Cooperstown," *Natural History* 98, no. 11 (November 1989): 24.

THE ART OF YELLOWSTONE

1. Wilkins, *Thomas Moran*, 63.
2. Langford, "Wonders, Part One," 6–7.
3. Langford, "Wonders, Part Two," 124.
4. Langford, "Wonders, Part Two," 124.

5. Gunnison, *Rambles Overland*, 11.

6. Hayden, *Preliminary Report*, 83–84.

7. William Henry Jackson, *Time Exposure* (Albuquerque: University of New Mexico Press, 1986), 200.

8. John Gibson, *Great Waterfalls, Cataracts, and Geysers* (London: T. Nelson, 1887).

9. F. K. Warren, ed., *California Illustrated* (Boston: DeWolfe, Fiske and Co., 1892) and Hezekiah Butterworth, *Zigzag Journeys in the Western States of America* (London: Dean and Son, n.d.).

10. Carrier, *Letters*, 123.

11. O. S. T. Drake, "A Lady's Trip to the Yellowstone Park," *Every Girl's Annual* (London: Hatchard's, 1887), 348.

EXPERIENCING YELLOWSTONE

1. Langford, "Wonders, Part Two," 117.

2. "The Yellowstone National Park," *Scribner's Monthly* 4, no. 1 (May 1872): 120.

3. Bradley in Ferdinand V. Hayden, *Sixth Annual Report of the United States Geological Survey of the Territories* (Washington, D.C.: GPO, 1873), 239.

4. Chittenden, *Yellowstone Park*, v.

5. Williams, "Vacation Notes," 11.

6. National Park Service, *Circulars of General Information: The National Parks* (Washington, D.C.: GPO, 1934), 1.

7. Erk, *Merry Crusade*, 119.

8. Thomas D. Murphy, *Three Wonderlands of the American West* (Boston: L. C. Page, 1912), 11.

9. Erk, *Merry Crusade*, 77.

10. Muir, *Our National Parks*, 52.

11. Nellie Meyer Ranney, "1905 Diary Entries Recall Rigors of Wagon Trip to Yellowstone Park: From the Diary of Nellie Meyer Ranney," ed. Charlotte Dehnert, *Wyoming State Journal*, 1 November 1979, n.p.

12. Wingate, *Through the Yellowstone*, 94.

13. C. J. Collins, *Yellowstone National Park* (Omaha, Nebr.: Union Pacific System, 1930), 6.

14. Charles W. Stoddard, "In Wonder-Land," *Ave Maria* (Notre Dame, Ind.) 47, no. 7 (August 1898): 202.

15. Drake, "A Lady's Trip," 347.

16. Kipling, *American Notes*, 98.

17. Strahorn, *Fifteen Thousand*, 272.

18. Erk, *Merry Crusade*, 66.

19. Mrs. James M. Hamilton, "Through Yellowstone in 1883 with Mrs. James Hamilton," Typewritten manuscript (Yellowstone Research Library, Mammoth Hot Springs, Wyo., 1967), 6.

20. Stoddard, *Lectures*, 222.

21. Olin D. Wheeler, *Wonderland 1903* (St. Paul, Minn.: Northern Pacific Railway, 1903), 40.

22. Washburn, *To the Pacific*, 168.

23. Gerrish, *World's Wonderland*, 234–35.

24. Mattoon, "Summer of 1889," 12–13.

25. Wylie, *Yellowstone*, 9.

26. Muir, *Our National Parks*, 56.

27. Stoddard, *Lectures*, 233.

28. John Sterling Yard in *Picturesque America*, ed. John Francis Kane (New York: Resorts and Playgrounds of America, 1925), 193.

29. A. B. Guptil, *Haynes Guide to Yellowstone Park* (St. Paul, Minn.: F. Jay Haynes, 1907), 32.

30. Jack E. Haynes, *Haynes Guide* (Bozeman, Mont.: Haynes Studios, 1949), 60.

31. Guptil, *Haynes Guide*, 47.

32. Haynes, *Haynes Guide*, 76.

33. Guptil, *Haynes Guide*, 38.

34. Haynes, *Haynes Guide*, 68.

35. Philetus W. Norris, *Annual Report of the Superintendent of Yellowstone National Park* (Washington, D.C.: GPO, 1880), 20.

36. Winser, *Great Northwest*, 17. These particular hot springs are not—nor were they ever—geysers. At Mammoth Hot Springs, the travertine limestone deposited by the springs is not strong enough to withstand the pressure necessary for a geyser eruption.

37. Kipling, *American Notes*, 93.

38. Wingate, *Through the Yellowstone*, 80.

39. C. F. Gordon Cumming, "The World's Wonderlands in Wyoming and New Zealand," *Overland Monthly* (2nd series) 5, no. 25 (January 1885): 11.

40. Doane, "Report of Lt. Doane," 14.

41. S. Weir Mitchell, "Through the Yellowstone Park to Fort Custer, Concluding Paper," *Lippincott's Magazine* 26 (July 1880): 33.

42. Norton, *Illustrated*, 14.

43. Norton in Strahorn, *Rockies and Beyond*, 208.

44. Raymond, *Camp and Cabin*, 189–90.

45. Barlow, "Reconnaissance," 10–11.

46. S. Weir Mitchell, "Through the Yellowstone Park to Fort Custer, Paper Number One," *Lippincott's Magazine* 25 (June 1880), 691–92.

47. Herman Haupt, *The Yellowstone National Park* (New York: J. M. Stoddart, 1883), 45.

48. Gibbon, "Wonders," 118.

49. Union Pacific System, *Geyserland*, 37.

50. Jean C. Sharpe, "A Yellowstone Story 1908–1917: This Is Me and This Is What I Remember," Manuscript (Yellowstone Research Library, Mammoth Hot Springs, Wyo., 1917), 5.

51. Northern Pacific Railroad, *The Way to Wonderland: Yellowstone National Park*. (St. Paul, Minn.: Northern Pacific Railway, 1935), 21–23.

52. W. S. Franklin, "The Yellowstone," *Science* 37, no. 951 (21 March, 1913): 447.

53. Gannett, *Sweet Land*, 172–73.

54. William S. Ellis, "The Pitfalls of Success," *National Geographic* 141, no. 5 (May 1972): 628.

55. Smith, *Trail*, 38–42.

56. Hayden, *Sixth Annual Report*, 53.

57. N. P. Langford, *The Discovery of Yellowstone Park*, ed. Aubrey L. Haines (Lincoln: University of Nebraska Press, 1972), 113.

58. Baker, "Marvels," 483.

59. Northern Pacific Railroad, *The Way*, 17.

60. Bradley in Hayden, *Sixth Annual Report*, 234.

61. Hugh M. Smith, "Mysterious Acoustic Phenomena in Yellowstone National Park," *Science* 63, no. 1641 (1926): 586.

62. Hiram M. Chittenden, *The Yellowstone National Park* (Cincinnati: Stewart and Kidd, 1915), 288–89; Edwin Linton, "Overhead Sounds of the Yellowstone Lake Region," *Science* 71, no. 1836 (1930): 98; and Riley, *Official Guide*, 69, respectively.

63. Haynes, *Haynes Guide*, 104.

THE IDEA OF THE IDEAL

1. Stephen Jay Gould, "Cordelia's Dilemma," *Natural History* 102, no. 2 (February 1991): 21.
2. Yi-Fu Tuan, "Space and Place: Humanistic Perspective" in *Philosophy in Geography*, ed. Stephen Gale and Gunnar Olsson (Boston: D. Reidel, 1979), 410.
3. Joseph L. Sax, "America's National Parks: Their Principles, Purposes, and Prospects," *Natural History* (October 1976): 81.
4. Roberts, *Shoshone*, 209.
5. Bartlett, *Wilderness Besieged*.
6. Edwin Kelsey, "Letter to Sister 'G', December 3, 1898," Letter (Yellowstone Research Library, Mammoth Hot Springs, Wyo., 1898).
7. Carrier, *Letters*, 123.
8. Strong, *A Trip*, 79.
9. Wheeler, *Wonderland '96*, 55–56.
10. Schullery, *Mountain Time*, 192.
11. N. P. Langford, Handwritten manuscript of lectures given by N. P. Langford during 1870–71 (Yellowstone Research Library, Mammoth Hot Springs, Wyo., c. 1870), 4.
12. Hayden, *Preliminary Report*, 54.
13. The Lions Club, *The Cody Road to Yellowstone Park* (Cody, Wyo.: Lions Club, 1920), 1.
14. Northern Pacific Railway, *The Way*, 49.
15. Charles Van Tassell, *Truthful Lies* (Bozeman, Mont.: C. Van Tassell, 1913), 23.
16. Carrie T. McLaughlin, *A Trip to Yellowstone Park in Horse and Buggy Days* (Published privately, 1904), 57.
17. Langford, "Wonders, Part One," 6–7.
18. Wheeler, *Wonderland '96*, 80.
19. Emerson Hough in *Haynes New Guide and Motorists' Complete Road Log of Yellowstone National Park*, ed. Jack E. Haynes (St. Paul, Minn.: J. E. Haynes, 1926), 112.
20. McLaughlin, *Horse and Buggy Days*, 87.
21. Thomas R. Vale, "No Romantic Landscapes for Our National Parks?" *Natural Areas Journal* 8, no. 2 (1988): 115–16.

.

Yellowstone Lake sunset

BIBLIOGRAPHY

Anderson, George. 1897. Work of the Cavalry in Protecting Yellowstone National Park. *Journal of the United States Cavalry Association* (March 1897). In Paul Schullery, *Old Yellowstone Days* (Boulder: Colorado Associated University Press, 1979), 173–81.

Andreae, A. 1893. Ueber die künstliche Nachamung des Geysirphänomens. *Neues Jahrbuch für Mineralogie, Geologie und Palaeontologie*, II.Band:1–18.

Augspurger, Marie M. 1948. *Yellowstone National Park: Historical and Descriptive*. Middletown, Ohio: Naegele-Auer Printing.

Ayer, I. Winslow. 1880. *Life in the Wilds of America, and Wonders of the West in and Beyond the Bounds of Civilization*. Grand Rapids, Iowa: Central Publishing.

Baker, Ray Stannard. 1903. A Place of Marvels: Yellowstone Park as It Now Is. *Century Magazine* 66(4):481–91.

Barlow, J. W., and D. P. Heap. 1872. *Report of a Reconnaissance of the Basin of the Upper Yellowstone in 1871*. 42nd Cong., 2nd sess., Sen. Exec. Doc. No. 66, 1–43.

Bassford, A., and Fryxell, Fritiof. 1967. *Home Thoughts from Afar*. East Hampton, N.Y.: East Hampton Free Library.

Bauer, Clyde Max. 1955. *Yellowstone—Its Underworld*. Washington, D.C.: National Park Service.

Beadle, J. H. 1873. *The Undeveloped West*. Philadelphia: National Publishing.

Beautiful America. 1924. *Beautiful America January 1925*. New York: Beautiful America Publishing.

Bell, Alfred and Estella. 1978. A Wedding Trip to Yellowstone: Summer of 1904. Edited by Amanda Bell Spitzer. Courtesy of the *Tonica News*, Tonica, Illinois. Yellowstone Research Library, Mammoth Hot Springs, Wyo.

Birney, Hoffman. 1930. *Roads to Roam*. Philadelphia: Penn Publishing.

Bohlin, K. J. 1893. *Genom den Stora Västern*. Stockholm: K. J. Bohlins Förlag.

Bolin, Luis A. 1962. *The National Parks of the United States*. New York: Alfred A. Knopf.

Borgh, Anna. 1988. Letter in *Yellowstone Park News* newsletter, no. 5 (December 1988): 2.

Brent, John. 1910. *The Empire of the West*. Omaha, Nebr.: Union Pacific Railroad.

Brockett, L. P. 1881. *Our Western Empire*. Philadelphia: Bradley.

Bromley, Isaac H. 1872. The Big Trees and the Yosemite. *Scribner's Monthly* 3(3):261–77.

Brückmann, Werner. 1948. *Du Ferner Westen*. Würzburg, Germany: Lothar Sauer-Morhard Verlag.

Bryant, William Cullen. 1872. *Picturesque America, or the Land We Live In*. 2 vols. New York: D. Appleton.

Bryce, James. 1913. *University and Historical Addresses*. New York: Macmillan.

Buffum, George Washington. 1885. Diary-Log of lumber wagon trip from Fort Collins, Colorado to Yellowstone National Park, summer of 1885. Yellowstone Research Library, Mammoth Hot Springs, Wyo.

Burroughs, John. 1907. *Camping and Tramping with Roosevelt*. Boston: Houghton Mifflin. In Paul Schullery, *Old Yellowstone Days* (Boulder: Colorado Associated University Press, 1979), 206–28.

———. 1909. Mit Präsident Roosevelt im Yellowstone-Park. *Kosmos* 6:121–27.

———. 1911. The Grand Cañon of the Colorado. *Century* 59(31):425–38.

Butcher, Devereux. 1947. *Exploring Our National Parks and Monuments*. New York: Oxford University Press.

Butterworth, Hezekiah. n.d. *Zigzag Journeys in the Western States of America*. London: Dean and Son.

Campbell, Marius R., et al. 1915. *Guidebook of the Western United States*. Part A: The Northern Pacific Route. Washington, D.C.: GPO.

Campbell, Reau. 1909. *Campbell's New Revised Complete Guide and Descriptive Book of the Yellowstone Park*. Chicago: E. M. Campbell.

———. 1913. *Campbell's New Revised Second Edition Complete Guide and Descriptive Book of the Yellowstone Park*. Chicago: H. E. Klamer.

———. 1914. *Campbell's New Revised Third Edition Complete Guide and Descriptive Book of the Yellowstone Park*. Chicago: H. E. Klamer.

———. 1923. *Campbell's New Revised Complete Guide and Descriptive Book of the Yellowstone Park*. Chicago: Cuneo-Henneberry.

Carpenter, Frank D. 1935. *Adventures in Geyserland*. Caldwell, Ind.: Caxton Printers.

Carrier, Jim. 1987. *Letters from Yellowstone*. Boulder: Roberts Rinehart.

Carter, Forest L. 1974. *Reminiscences of an Old Yellowstone Ranger between the Years 1921 and 1926*. Grand Marais, Mich.: Grand Sable Publishing.

Chaney, Jack. 1928. *Foolish Questions*. Lincoln, Nebr.: Woodruff Press.

Chapple, Joe. 1922. *A'Top o' the World*. Boston: Chapple Publishing.

Chatterton, Fenimore, ed. 1899. *The State of Wyoming*. Cheyenne, Wyo.: S. A. Bristol.

———. 1901. *The State of Wyoming*. Cheyenne, Wyo.: S. A. Bristol.

———. 1904. *The State of Wyoming*. Cheyenne: S. A. Bristol.

Chittenden, Hiram Martin. 1895. *The Yellowstone National Park: Historical and Descriptive*. Cincinnati: R. Clarke.

———. 1915. *The Yellowstone National Park*. Cincinnati: Stewart and Kidd.

———. 1961. *Being a Selection from His Unpublished Journals, Diaries and Reports*. Edited by Bruce LeRay. Tacoma, Wash.: Washington State Historical Society.

———. 1964. *The Yellowstone National Park*. Edited by Richard A. Bartlett. Norman: University of Oklahoma Press.

Clampitt, J. W. 1889. *Echoes from the Rocky Mountains*. Chicago: Belford, Clarke.

Clawson, Cal C. 1872. The Region of the Wonderful Lake—Yellowstone. A series of articles in the *New Northwest* (Deer Lodge, Mont.), December 2 and 16, 1871; January 13 and 27, 1872; February 10 and 24, 1872; May 18, 1872.

Cleland, A. M. 1910. *Through Wonderland*. Chicago: Rand McNally.

Cockhill, Brian, ed. 1972. The Quest of Warren Gillette: Based on the Original Diary. *Montana* 22(3):12–30.

Collins, C. J. 1930. *Yellowstone National Park*. Omaha, Nebr.: Union Pacific System.

Cook, Charles W., David E. Folsom, and William Peterson. 1965. *The Valley of the Upper Yellowstone*. Edited by Aubrey L. Haines. Norman: University of Oklahoma Press.

Cook, Joel. 1900. *America: Picturesque and Descriptive*. 3 vols. Philadelphia: Henry J. Coastes.

Corthell, N. E. 1928. *A Family Trek to the Yellowstone*. Laramie, Wyo.: Laramie Printing.

Cox, James. 1888. *My Native Land*. St. Louis, Mo.: Blair Publishing.

———. 1894. *Our Own Country*. St. Louis, Mo.: National.

Craighead, Karen, and Derek Craighead. 1972. A Walk through the Wilderness. *National Geographic* 141(5):579–603.

Credner, H. 1895. Der National-Park am Yellowstone. *Geographischer Zeitschrift* 1:79–89.

Cruikshank, Margaret Andrews. 1989. A Lady's Trip to Yellowstone in 1883: Earth Could Not Furnish Another Such Sight. Edited by Lee H. Whittlesey. *Montana* 39(1):2–15.

Cumming, C. F. Gordon. 1885. The World's Wonderlands in Wyoming and New Zealand. *Overland Monthly* (Second Series) 5(25):1–13.

Cundall, Alan W., and Herbert T. Lystrup. 1969. *Yellowstone National Park*. West Yellowstone, Mont.: Hamilton Stores.

Dexter, Mary Reeves. 1889. Handwritten letters dated July 28, July 30, and August 2, 1889, in Special Collections, Montana State University Library, Bozeman, Mont.

Dickey, Emerson. Excerpts from Journal, July 1932. Yellowstone Research Library, Mammoth Hot Springs, Wyo.

Doane, Gustavus C. 1871. *The Report of Lieutenant Gustavus C. Doane upon the So-Called Yellowstone Expedition of 1870*. 41st Cong., 3rd sess., Sen. Exec. Doc. No. 51, 1–40.

Donaldson, Rose Simon. 1925. My First Trip to Yellowstone Park, 1925. Yellowstone Research Library, Mammoth Hot Springs, Wyo.

Douglass, Irwin B. 1936–1939. Notes of a Summer Naturalist. Handwritten notes in Yellowstone Research Library, Mammoth Hot Springs, Wyo.

Drake, O. S. T. 1887. A Lady's Trip to the Yellowstone Park. *Every Girl's Annual* (London: Hatchard's), 346–49.

Dumbell, K. E. M. 1914. *California and the Far West*. New York: James Pott.

Dunraven, Earl of. 1876. *The Great Divide*. London: Chatto and Windus.

Edwards, Guy D. 1933. Yellowstone National Park in Montana Department of Agriculture, Labor and Industry's *Montana Resources and Opportunities Edition of 1933* VII(IV):37–38.

Ehrlich, Gretel. 1991. The Volcano Sleeps as We Play. *Traveler,* August, 100–105, 114.

Ellis, William S. 1972. The Pitfalls of Success. *National Geographic* 141(5):616–31.

Ellsworth, Fred W. 1912. Through Yellowstone Park with the American Institute of Banking. *Moody Magazine* 14(5):366–75.

Erk, Edmund Frederick. 1906. *A Merry Crusade to the Golden Gate*. Akron, Ohio: Werner.

Everts, Truman C. 1904. Thirty Seven Days of Peril. *Contributions to the Historical Society of Montana* 5:395–427.

Faris, John T. 1934. *Roaming American Playgrounds*. New York: Farrar and Rinehart.

Fennell, James Carson. 1892. In the Yellowstone Park. *The California Illustrated Magazine* 2(3):348–63.

Fenneman, N. M. 1913. The Yellowstone National Park. *Journal of Geography* 11:314–20.

Ferris, W. A. 1940. *Life in the Rocky Mountains 1830–1835*. Edited by Paul C. Phillips. Denver: Old West Publishing.

Folsom, David E. 1904. The Folsom-Cook Exploration of the Upper Yellowstone in the Year 1869. *Contributions to the Historical Society of Montana* 5:348–69.

Fountain, Paul. 1906. *The Eleven Eaglets of the West.* London: John Murray.

Franklin, W. S. 1913. The Yellowstone. *Science* 37(951):446–47.

Frazer, Elizabeth. 1920. The Last Wilderness. *Saturday Evening Post,* January 24, 14–15, 141, 145, 149, 153, 156.

Freeman, Lewis R. 1923. *Down the Yellowstone.* London: William Heinemann.

Frost, Ned. 1929. Going through the Park. *Saturday Evening Post,* March 30, 35–37, 121, 124, 127.

Gannett, Henry. 1898. *North America. Volume II: The United States.* London: Edward Stanford.

Gannett, L. 1934. *Sweet Land.* Garden City, N.Y.: Doubleday, Doran and Co.

Garden and Forest. 1888. Editorial. *Garden and Forest,* April 4, 75.

———. 1890. Protection of the Yellowstone Park. *Garden and Forest,* December 10, 593.

———. 1891. Yellowstone National Park. *Garden and Forest,* December 16, 589–90.

———. 1892. The Yellowstone Park Company. *Garden and Forest,* March 2, 98.

———. 1892. Editorial. *Garden and Forest,* March 9, 120.

———. 1892. The Boundaries of Yellowstone Park. *Garden and Forest,* May 25, 241.

———. 1894. The Yellowstone National Park. *Garden and Forest,* April 4, 131.

———. 1894. Yellowstone Park. *Garden and Forest,* April 18, 151–52.

Garvens-Garvensburg, Wolfgang von. 1910. Wild im Yellowstone-Park. *Kosmos* 7:52–54.

Gates, Charles H. 1903. *Yellowstone National Park, Alaska and the White Pass.* Toledo, Ohio: Franklin Printing.

Geikie, Archibald. 1892. *Geological Sketches at Home and Abroad.* New York: Macmillan.

Gerrish, Theodore. 1887. *Life in the World's Wonderland.* Biddleford, Maine (published privately).

Gibbon, John. 1873. The Wonders of the Yellowstone. *Journal of the American Geographical Society of New York* 5(99):112–37.

Gibson, John. 1887. *Great Waterfalls, Cataracts, and Geysers.* London: T. Nelson and Sons.

Grant, Roland Dwight. 1908. Changes in the Yellowstone Park. *Bulletin of the American Geographical Society* 40(5):277–82.

Gray, John S. 1972. Trials of a Trailblazer: P. W. Norris and Yellowstone. *Montana Magazine of Western History* 22(3):54–63.

Grinnell, George Bird. 1972. *The Passing of the Great West.* Edited by John F. Reiger. New York: Winchester.

Gunnison, Almon. 1884. *Rambles Overland.* Boston: Universalist Publishing.

Guptill, A. B. 1890. *Practical Guide to Yellowstone National Park.* St. Paul, Minn.: Pioneer Press.

———. 1892. *A Ramble in Wonderland.* St. Paul, Minn.: Northern Pacific Railroad.

———. 1894. *Yellowstone Park Guide.* St. Paul, Minn.: H. L. Collins.

———. 1900. *Haynes Guide to Yellowstone Park.* St. Paul, Minn.: H. L. Collins.

———. 1907. *Haynes Guide to the Yellowstone Park.* St. Paul, Minn.: Pioneer Press.

———. 1908. *Haynes Guide to the Yellowstone Park.* St. Paul, Minn.: Pioneer Press.

Hague, Arnold. 1913. Yellowstone National Park. *American Forestry* 19(5):300–17.

Hamilton, Mrs. James M. 1967. Through Yellowstone in 1883 with Mrs. James Hamilton. Typewritten manuscript. Yellowstone Research Library, Mammoth Hot Springs, Wyo.

Harrison, Carter H. 1891. *A Summer's Outing and the Old Man's Story.* Chicago: Donohue, Henneberry.

Hassell, Richard Burton. 1928. A Trip to the Yellowstone 49 Years Ago. Yellowstone Research Library, Mammoth Hot Springs, Wyo.

Hatch, Rufus. 1882. A Summer Souvenir: "Uncle Rufus" and "Ma." *The New Northwest* (Deer Lodge, Mont.).

Hatfield, W. F. 1905. *"Geyserland and Wonderland": A View and Guidebooks of the Yellowstone National Park.* St. Anthony, Ind.: W. F. Hatfield.

Haupt, Herman. 1883. *The Yellowstone National Park.* New York: J. M. Stoddart.

Hayden, Ferdinand V. 1872a. *Preliminary Report of the U.S. Geological Survey of Montana and Portions of Adjacent Territories; Being a Fifth Annual Report of Progress.* Washington, D.C.: GPO.

———. 1872b. The Wonders of the West—II. *Scribner's Monthly* 3(4):388–96.

———. 1873. *Sixth Annual Report of the United States Geological Survey of the Territories.* Washington, D.C.: GPO.

———. 1876. Address of Dr. F. V. Hayden, U.S. Geologist: The Great West and the Scenery of Our National Parks, April 15, 1874. *Journal of the American Geographical Society of New York* 6(48):196–211.

———. 1879. The Yellowstone Park in F. E. Shearer's *The Pacific Tourist.* New York: Adams and Bishop, 161–76.

———. 1880. *The Great West.* Bloomington, Ill.: Charles R. Brodix.

———. 1883. *Twelfth Annual Report of the U.S. Geological and Geographical Survey of the Territories.* Washington, D.C.: GPO.

Haynes, F. Jay. 1912. *Haynes Official Guide: Yellowstone National Park.* St. Paul, Minn.: Pioneer.

Haynes, Jack E. 1916. *Haynes Guide: The Complete Handbook.* St. Paul, Minn.: J. E. Haynes.

———. 1920. *The Motorists' Complete Road Log of Yellowstone National Park.* St. Paul, Minn.: J. E. Haynes.

———. 1921. *Haynes New Guide and Motorists' Complete Road Log of Yellowstone National Park.* St. Paul, Minn.: J. E. Haynes.

———. 1926. *Haynes New Guide and Motorists' Complete Road Log of Yellowstone National Park.* St. Paul: J. E. Haynes.

———. 1929. *Haynes New Guide and Motorists' Complete Road Log of Yellowstone National Park.* Yellowstone Park, Wyo.: Haynes Picture Shops.

———. 1934. *Haynes New Guide: The Complete Handbook of Yellowstone National Park.* Yellowstone National Park: Haynes Picture Shops.

———. 1939. *Haynes Guide.* Yellowstone Park, Wyo.: Haynes.

———. 1942. The First Winter Trip through Yellowstone National Park. *Annals of Wyoming* 14(2):88–97.

———. 1946. *Haynes Guide.* Yellowstone Park, Wyo.: Haynes.

———. 1949. *Haynes Guide.* Bozeman, Mont.: Haynes Studios.

———. 1952. *Haynes Guide.* Bozeman, Mont.: Haynes Studios.

———. 1955. *Haynes Guide.* Bozeman, Mont.: Haynes Studios.

———. 1957. *Haynes Guide.* Bozeman, Mont.: Haynes Studios.

———. 1958. *Haynes Guide.* Bozeman, Mont.: Haynes Studios.

Hedges, Cornelius. 1904. Journal of Judge Cornelius Hedges. *Contributions to the Historical Society of Montana* 5:370–94.

Heuschkel, Julius, E. George Markin, Glenn F. Muchow, Leverett G. Richards, and Frank B. Wisner. 1925. Yellowstone 1925. Photo album with captions in Yellowstone Research Library, Mammoth Hot Springs, Wyo.

Hochstetter, Ferdinand von. 1863. *Neu=Seeland.* Stuttgart, Germany: Cotta'scher Verlag.

Holmes, Burton. 1901. *The Burton Holmes Lectures.* Battle Creek, Mich.: Little-Preston.

Hough, Emerson. 1894. Forest and Stream's Yellowstone Park Game Exploration. *Forest and Stream,* May 5, in Paul Schullery, ed., *Old Yellowstone Days* (Boulder: Colorado Associated University Press, 1979), 129–44.

————. 1929. *Maw's Vacation*. St. Paul, Minn.: Haynes Picture Shops.

————. 1919. An Appreciation of Yellowstone National Park in U.S. Railroad Administration's *National Park Service Series*. Bound collection of 13 pamphlets.

Hoyt, Colgate. 1986. "Roughing It up the Yellowstone to Wonderland": An Account of a Trip through the Yellowstone Valley in 1878. Edited by Carroll Van West. *Montana Magazine of Western History* 36(2):22–35.

Hyde, John. 1886. A Description of the Country Traversed by the Northern Pacific Railroad. In F. Schwatka, *Wonderland; or Alaska and the Inland Passage* (St. Paul, Minn.: Northern Pacific Railroad, 1886).

————. 1888. *Wonderland; or the Pacific Northwest and Alaska*. St. Paul, Minn.: Northern Pacific Railroad.

James, George Wharton. 1915. *Our American Wonderlands*. Chicago: A. C. McClurg.

Jeffers, Le Roy. 1923. *The Call of the Mountains*. New York: Dodd, Mead and Co.

Johnson, Clifton. 1910. *Highways and Byways*. New York: Macmillan.

Johnson, Mrs. Edward H. 1905. Diary of a Trip through Yellowstone Park, 1905. Typewritten manuscript at Yellowstone Park Research Library, Mammoth Hot Springs, Wyo.

Jones, O. T. 1929. In the Yellowstone with Princeton, *Nature* 123(3109):852–55.

Jones, William A. 1875. *Report upon the Reconnaissance of Northwestern Wyoming Including Yellowstone National Park Made in the Summer of 1873*. Washington, D.C.: GPO.

Kane, John Francis, ed. 1925. *Picturesque America*. New York: Resorts and Playgrounds of America.

Kelsey, Edwin. 1898. Letter to Sister "G," December 3, 1898. Yellowstone Research Library, Mammoth Hot Springs, Wyo.

Kenney, R. D. c. 1926. *From Geyserdom to Show-me Land*. Clyde Park, Mont.: R. D. Kenney.

Kipling, Rudyard. 1981. *American Notes*. Edited by Arrell Morgan Gibson. Norman: University of Oklahoma Press.

————. 1979. In Paul Schullery, ed., *Old Yellowstone Days* (Boulder: Colorado Associated University Press, 1979), 84–114.

Kirk, Henry A. 1972. Sixty Days to and in Yellowstone Park. Edited by Daniel Y. Meschter. *Annals of Wyoming* 44(1):5–23.

Kronen, May. 1904. Trip to the Yellowstone National Park, July and August 1907. Typewritten manuscript in possession of family.

Langford, Nathaniel P. 1871a. The Wonders of the Yellowstone, Part One. *Scribner's Monthly* 2(1):1–17.

————. 1871b. The Wonders of the Yellowstone, Part Two. *Scribner's Monthly* 2(2):113–29.

————. 1873. The Ascent of Mount Hayden. *Scribner's Monthly* 6(2):129–57.

————. 1972. *The Discovery of Yellowstone Park*. Edited by Aubrey L. Haines. Lincoln: University of Nebraska Press.

Lawrence, O. C. 1938. The Old and the New. Typewritten account of travel to Yellowstone National Park in 1909 and 1938. Special Collections, Montana State University Library, Bozeman, Mont.

Leclercq, Jules. 1886. *La Terre des Merveilles*. Paris: Librairie Hachette et Cie.

Leslie, Mrs. Frank. 1877. *California: A Pleasure Trip from Gotham to the Golden Gate*. New York: G. W. Carleton.

Lincoln, Andrew Carey. 1913. *Motorcycle Chums in Yellowstone Park*. Chicago: M. A. Donohue.

Linton, Edwin. 1930. Overhead Sounds of the Yellowstone Lake Region. *Science* 71(1836): 97–99.

Lohse, Joyce B. 1988. *A Yellowstone Savage*. Colorado Springs: J. D. Charles Publishing.

Ludlow, William. 1876. *Report of a Reconnaissance from Carroll, Montana Territory, on the Upper*

Missouri, to the Yellowstone National Park, and Return, Made in the Summer of 1875. Washington, D.C.: GPO.

Marron, Carol. 1988. *Yellowstone.* Mankato, Minn.: Crestwood House.

Marston, Edward. 1886. *Frank's Ranche or My Holiday in the Rockies.* London: Sampson Low, Marston, Searle, and Rivington.

Marx, George S. 1898. Yellowstone Park. In Charles W. Burdick, *The State of Wyoming* (Cheyenne, Wyo.: Sun-Leader Printing House), 140.

Mattoon, A. M. 1917. The Yellowstone National Park, Summer of 1889. Handwritten journal. Yellowstone Research Library, Mammoth Hot Springs, Wyo.

McElrath, Thomson P. 1880. *The Yellowstone Valley.* St. Paul, Minn.: Pioneer Press.

McLaughlin, Carrie Todd. 1943. *A Trip to Yellowstone Park in Horse and Buggy Days.* (Published privately).

Melbo, Irving R. 1941. *Our Country's National Parks.* Indianapolis: Bobbs-Merrill.

Mitchell, S. Weir. 1880a. Through the Yellowstone Park to Fort Custer. Paper Number One. *Lippincott's Magazine* 25:688–704.

———. 1880b. Through the Yellowstone Park to Fort Custer. Concluding Paper. *Lippincott's Magazine* 26:29–41.

Montana Bureau of Agriculture, Labor and Industry. 1899. *"The Treasure State": Montana and Its Magnificent Resources 1898.* Helena, Mont.: Independent Publishing.

———. 1928. *Montana Resources and Opportunities Edition* 3(2). Helena, Mont.: Naegele Printing.

Montana Department of Agriculture and Publicity. 1914. *The Resources and Opportunities of Montana.* Helena, Mont.: Independent Publishing.

———. 1918. *Resources and Opportunities of Montana.* Helena, Mont.: Independent Publishing.

———. 1919. *Resources of Montana.* Helena, Mont.: Independent Publishing.

———. 1920. *Resources of Montana.* Helena, Mont.: Independent Publishing.

Montana Department of Publicity of the Bureau of Agriculture, Labor and Industry. 1909. *Montana.* Helena, Mont.: Independent Publishing.

———. 1912. *Montana.* Helena, Mont.: Independent Publishing.

Montana World's Fair Commission. 1904. *Montana the Treasure State.* St. Louis, Mo.: Con. P. Curran Printing.

Muench, Joyce and Josef Muench. 1949. *Along Yellowstone and Grand Teton Trails.* New York: Hastings House.

Muir, John. 1981. *Our National Parks.* Madison: University of Wisconsin Press.

Murphy, Thomas D. 1912. *Three Wonderlands of the American West.* Boston: L. C. Page.

Mushbach, J. E. 1878. Diary of J. E. Mushbach, 1878. Handwritten manuscript. Yellowstone Research Library, Mammoth Hot Springs, Wyo.

National Park Service. 1918. *General Information Circulars: National Parks and Monuments 1918.* Washington, D.C.: GPO.

———. 1920–1927. The National Parks, Season of 1920–1927. *Rules and Regulations.* Washington, D.C.: GPO.

———. 1928. *Circulars of General Information: The National Parks.* Washington, D.C.: GPO.

———. 1934. *Circulars of General Information: The National Parks.* Washington, D.C.: GPO.

———. 1939. *Circulars of General Information: The National Parks.* Washington, D.C.: GPO.

———. 1940. *Circulars of General Information: The National Parks.* Washington, D.C.: GPO.

Norris, Philetus W. 1880a. *Annual Report of the Superintendent of Yellowstone National Park.* Washington, D.C.: GPO.

———. 1880b. Map of the Yellowstone National Park with the Adjacent Hoodoo Region. Washington, D.C.: Department of the Interior.

———. 1884. *Calumet of the Coteau*. Philadelphia: J. B. Lippincott.

Northern Pacific Railroad. 1882. *The Climate, Soil and Resources of the Yellowstone Valley*. St. Paul, Minn.: Pioneer Press.

———. 1909. *The Land of Geysers*. St. Paul, Minn.: Northern Pacific Railway.

———. 1914. Advertisement in *The Journal of Geography* 11(10):n.p.

Northern Pacific Railway. c. 1935. *The Way to Wonderland: Yellowstone National Park*. St. Paul, Minn.: Northern Pacific Railway.

Northern Pacific Railway Company. n.d. *Yellowstone National Park*. Minneapolis, Minn.: Bloom Brothers.

Northern Pacific Railway and Burlington Route. 1933. *Magic Yellowstone*. St. Paul, Minn.: Northern Pacific Railway.

Norton, Harry J. 1873. *Wonderland Illustrated; or, Horseback Rides through the Yellowstone National Park*. Virginia City, Mont.: Harry J. Norton.

Olmstead, Frederick Law. 1952. The Yosemite Valley and the Mariposa Big Trees. Edited by Laura Roper. *Landscape Architecture* 43(1):14–23.

Osmond, Mable Cross. 1874. Memories of a Trip through Yellowstone Park in 1874. Typewritten copy of the original manuscript at Yellowstone Research Library, Mammoth Hot Springs, Wyo.

Overland Monthly. 1917. A Ten Minute Trip through Yellowstone Park. *Overland Monthly* 70(2):101–12.

Owen, William O. 1891. The First Bicycle Tour of the Yellowstone National Park. *Outing*, June, 191–95.

Panton, Samuel P. 1986. Surveying in Yellowstone National Park, 1882. *Montana* 36(2):72–76.

Paull, Caroline L. 1897. Notes on Yellowstone National Park, June 28–August 4, 1897. Manuscript at Yellowstone Research Library, Mammoth Hot Springs, Wyo.

Peattie, Elia W. 1890. *A Journey through Wonderland*. St. Paul, Minn.: Northern Pacific Railroad.

Pierce, Flora Chase. 1897. Letter dated August 8, 1897. Yellowstone Park Research Library, Mammoth Hot Springs, Wyo.

Pierrepont, Edward. 1884. *Fifth Avenue to Alaska*. New York: G. P. Putnam.

Price, Rose Lambert. 1898. *A Summer in the Rockies*. London: Sampson Low, Marston, and Co.

Quick, Herbert. 1911. *Yellowstone Nights*. Indianapolis: Bobbs-Merrill.

Quinn, Vernon. 1923. *Beautiful America*. New York: Frederick A. Stokes.

Raftery, John H. 1912. *A Miracle in Hotel Building*. Mammoth Hot Springs, Wyo.: Yellowstone Park.

———. 1943. Historical Sketch of Yellowstone National Park. *Annals of Wyoming* 15(2):101–32.

Ranney, Nellie Meyer. 1979. 1905 Diary Entries Recall Rigors of Wagon Trip to Yellowstone Park. From the diary of Nellie Meyer Ranney. Edited by Charlotte Dehnert. *Wyoming State Journal*, November 1.

Raymond, Rossiter. 1880. *Camp and Cabin*. New York: Fords, Howard, and Hulbert.

Reik, Henry Ottridge. 1920. *A Tour of America's National Parks*. New York: E. P. Dutton.

Remington, Frederic. 1898. Chapter 6: Frederic Remington, 1893. In Paul Schullery, ed., *Old Yellowstone Days* (Boulder: Colorado Associated University Press, 1979), 116–27.

Richardson, James. 1873. *Wonders of the Yellowstone*. New York: Scribner, Armstrong.

———. 1876. *Wonders of the Yellowstone Region*. London: Blackie and Son.

Riley, W. C. 1889. *Official Guide to the Yellowstone National Park*. St. Paul, Minn.: W. C. Riley.

Roberts, Edwards. 1888. *Shoshone and Other Western Wonders*. New York: Harper.

Rodenbaugh, Theo. F. 1875. From Everglade to Cañon with the Second Dragoons. New York: D. Van Nostrand.

Rolfe, Mary A. 1928. *Our National Parks*. Book Two. New York: Benj. H. Sanborn.

Roosevelt, Theodore. 1923. Wilderness Reserves: The Yellowstone National Park. In Paul

Schullery, *Old Yellowstone Days* (Boulder: Colorado Associated University Press, 1979), 182–205.

Roylance, Ward J. 1953. *Rainbow Roads Guide to Highways 91, 89, and 191*. Salt Lake City: Rainbow Roads.

Russell, Osborne. 1965. *Journal of a Trapper 1834–1843*. Edited by Aubrey L. Haines. Lincoln: University of Nebraska Press.

Rutgers, Lispenard. 1894. *On and off the Saddle*. New York: G. P. Putnam.

Scharff, Robert. 1966. *Yellowstone and Grand Teton National Parks*. New York: David McKay.

Scharr, Barbara Ann. 1926. The Wonderland of Today. *Montana Resources and Opportunities Edition*, 1928, Department of Agriculture, Labor and Industry 1(2):209–212.

Scholly, Dan R. 1991. *Guardians of the Yellowstone*. New York: William Morrow.

Schullery, Paul. 1988. *Mountain Time*. New York: Simon and Schuster.

Schwatka, Frederick. 1886. *Wonderland*. St. Paul, Minn.: Northern Pacific Railroad.

Scribner's Monthly. 1872. The Yellowstone National Park. *Scribner's Monthly* 4(1):120–21.

Sharpe, Jean C. 1917. A Yellowstone Story 1908–1917: This Is Me and This Is What I Remember. Manuscript at Yellowstone National Research Library, Mammoth Hot Springs, Wyo.

Skinner, M. P. 1924. *The Yellowstone Nature Book*. Chicago: A. C. McClurg.

———. 1925. *Bears in the Yellowstone*. Chicago: A. C. McClurg.

Smith, Hugh M. 1926. Mysterious Acoustic Phenomena in Yellowstone National Park. *Science* 63(1641):586–87.

Smith, Huntington. 1953. Tourists Who Act Like Pigs. *Saturday Evening Post,* May 30, 36–37, 80, 82–84.

Smith, Wallace. 1924. *On the Trail in Yellowstone*. New York: G. P. Putnam.

Stanley, Edwin J. 1880. *Rambles in Wonderland*. New York: D. Appleton.

Steel, Byron. 1947. *Let's Visit Our National Parks*. New York: Robert M. McBride.

Steele, David M. 1917. *Going Abroad Overland*. New York: G. P. Putnam.

Stewart, Donald C. 1989. *My Yellowstone Years*. Fowlerville, Mich.: Wilderness Adventure Books.

Stoddard, Charles Warren. 1898. In Wonder-Land. *Ave Maria* (Notre Dame, Ind. university newspaper) 47, nos. 6–11:172–75, 201–3, 237–41, 257–61, 295–99, 326–30.

Stoddard, John L. 1898. *John L. Stoddard's Lectures*. Vol. 10. Boston: Balch Brothers.

Story, Isabelle F. 1941. *Glimpses of Our National Parks*. Washington, D.C.: GPO.

Strahorn, Carrie Adell. 1911. *Fifteen Thousand Miles by Stage*. New York: G. P. Putnam.

Strahorn, Robert E. 1881a. *The Enchanted Land*. Omaha, Nebr.: New West Publishing.

———. 1881b. *To the Rockies and Beyond*. Chicago: Belford, Clarke, and Co.

Strong, William Emerson. 1968. *A Trip to the Yellowstone National Park*. Edited by Richard A. Bartlett. Norman: University of Oklahoma Press.

Sutton, Ann and Myron Sutton. c. 1972. *Yellowstone: A Century of the Wilderness Idea*. New York: Chanticleer Press.

Sweet, Elnathan. 1912. Horseback in Yellowstone Park. *Country Life in America* 2:88–89.

Synge, Georgina M. 1892. *A Ride through Wonderland*. London: Sampson Low.

Taylor, Bayard. 1859. *At Home and Abroad*. New York: G. P. Putnam.

Taylor, Charles M. 1901. *Touring Alaska and the Yellowstone*. Philadelphia: George W. Jacobs.

Taylor, E. O. 1885. Notes of a Trip to Yellowstone National Park. Handwritten diary in Special Collections, Montana State University, Bozeman, Mont.

Thane, Eric. 1950. *The Majestic Land: Peaks, Parks and Prevaricators of the Rockies and Highland Northwest*. Indianapolis: Bobbs-Merrill.

Thayer, William M. 1888. *Marvels of the New West*. Norwich, Conn.: Henry Bill Publishing.

———. 1891. *Marvels of the New West*. Norwich, Conn.: Henry Bill Publishing.

Tilden, Freeman. c. 1954. *The Fifth Essence*. Washington, D.C.: The National Park Trust Fund Board.

Topping, E. S. 1883. *Chronicles of the Yellowstone*. St. Paul, Minn.: Pioneer Press.

Trager, Martelle. 1939. *National Parks of the Northwest*. New York: Dodd, Mead and Co.

Trumbull, Walter. 1871a. The Washburn Yellowstone Expedition. Number One. *Overland Monthly* 6(5):431–37.

———. 1871b. The Washburn Yellowstone Expedition. Number Two. *Overland Monthly* 6(6):489–96.

Turpin, Frances Lynn. 1895. A Trip through Yellowstone Park, 1895. Typewritten manuscript in Special Collections, Montana State University Library, Bozeman, Mont.

Turrill, Gardner Stilson. 1901. *A Tale of the Yellowstone*. Jefferson, Iowa: G. S. Turrill Publishing.

Tweedy, Frank. 1888. The Forests of Yellowstone National Park. *Garden and Forest* 1:129–130.

Union Pacific System. 1924. *Geyserland*. Omaha, Nebr.: W. H. Murray.

United States Railroad Administration. 1919. *Yellowstone National Park*. Chicago: Rand McNally.

Van Tassell, Charles. 1913. *"Truthful Lies."* Bozeman, Mont.: C. Van Tassell.

Victor, Frances Fuller. 1974. *The River of the West*. Oakland, Calif.: Brooks-Sterling.

Vosburgh, Frederick G. 1959. Yellowstone National Park. *America's Wonderland*. Washington, D.C.: National Geographic Society, 59–83.

Warner, Charles. 1897. Editor's Study. *Harper's New Monthly Magazine*. In Paul Schullery, *Old Yellowstone Days* (Boulder: Colorado Associated University Press, 1979), 159–74.

Warren, F. K., ed. c. 1892. *California Illustrated*. Boston: DeWolfe, Fiske and Co.

Washburn, Henry D. 1871. *Report on Mining Statistics West of the Rocky Mountains*. Edited by R. W. Raymond, 1871, 42nd Cong., 1st Sess., House Exec. Doc. No. 10, 213–16.

Washburn, J. A. I. 1887. *To the Pacific and Back*. New York: Sunshine Publishing.

Weikert, Andrew J. 1900. Journal of the Tour through the Yellowstone National Park in August and September, 1877. *Contributions to the Historical Society of Montana* 3:152–74.

Wheeler, Olin D. 1893. *6,000 Miles through Wonderland*. St. Paul, Minn.: Northern Pacific Railroad.

———. 1895. *Sketches of Wonderland*. St. Paul, Minn.: Northern Pacific Railroad.

———. 1896. *Wonderland '96*. St. Paul, Minn.: Northern Pacific Railroad.

———. 1897. *Wonderland '97*. St. Paul, Minn.: Northern Pacific Railway.

———. 1898. *Wonderland '98*. St. Paul, Minn.: Northern Pacific Railway.

———. 1899. *Wonderland '99*. St. Paul, Minn.: Northern Pacific Railway.

———. 1900. *Wonderland 1900*. St. Paul, Minn.: Northern Pacific Railway.

———. 1901. *Wonderland 1901*. St. Paul, Minn.: Northern Pacific Railway.

———. 1902. *Wonderland 1902*. St. Paul, Minn.: Northern Pacific Railway.

———. 1903. *Wonderland 1903*. St. Paul, Minn.: Northern Pacific Railway.

———. 1904. *Wonderland 1904*. St. Paul, Minn.: Northern Pacific Railway.

———. 1905. *Wonderland 1905*. St. Paul, Minn.: Northern Pacific Railway.

———. 1906. *Wonderland 1906*. St. Paul, Minn.: Northern Pacific Railway.

White, Alma. 1933. *With God in the Yellowstone*. Zarephath, N.J.: Pillar of Fire.

White, Zillah Pocick. 1986. Handwritten letter. Yellowstone Research Library, Mammoth Hot Springs, Wyo.

Williams, J. E. 1888. Vacation Notes: Summer of 1888 (Through the Yellowstone Park), *Amherst* (Mass.) *Record,* September 26, 1–52.

Wingate, George W. 1886. *Through the Yellowstone Park on Horseback*. New York: O. Judd.

Winser, Henry J. 1883a. *The Great Northwest*. New York: G. P. Putnam.

———. 1883b. *The Yellowstone National Park: A Manual for Tourists*. New York: G. P. Putnam.

Wister, Owen. 1936. Old Yellowstone Days. *Harper's Monthly Magazine* 172:471–80.

———. 1958. *Owen Wister out West*. Edited by Fanny Kemble Wister. Chicago: University of Chicago Press.

Wolfe, Thomas. 1951. *A Western Journal*. Pittsburgh: University of Pittsburgh Press.

Wylie, William H., and Sara King Wiley. 1892. *The Yosemite, Alaska, and the Yellowstone*. New York: John Wiley.

Wylie, W. W. 1882. *Yellowstone National Park*. Kansas City, Mo.: Ramsey, Millett and Hudson.

Yard, Robert Sterling. 1917. *The National Parks Portfolio*. Washington, D.C.: GPO.

Yeager, Dorr G. 1947. *Your Western National Parks*. New York: Dodd, Mead and Co.

Zardetti, Otto. 1897. *Westlich! oder Durch den fernen Westen Nord-Amerikas*. Mainz, Denmark: Verlag von Franz Kirchheim.